T0354391

PHYSICAL PREPARATION
FOR ICE HOCKEY

BIOLOGICAL PRINCIPLES
AND PRACTICAL SOLUTIONS

ANTHONY DONSKOV

authorHOUSE®

AuthorHouse™
1663 Liberty Drive
Bloomington, IN 47403
www.authorhouse.com
Phone: 1 (800) 839-8640

Published by AuthorHouse   02/10/2017

ISBN: 978-1-5246-5122-0 (sc)
ISBN: 978-1-5246-5120-6 (hc)
ISBN: 978-1-5246-5121-3 (e)

Library of Congress Control Number: 2016919716

Print information available on the last page.

Photo courtesy of Ross Dettman Photography Ltd and the Chicago Wolves.

Foreword

It is an honor to write a forward for my best friend, someone I have grown up with and shared so many of my life experiences with, someone whom I truly believe in and has contributed personally and professionally to my own growth and development, someone whom I deeply care about – respect, admire, and trust, and someone who is a teacher, coach and mentor to others. My brother Anthony is truly an inspiration in my life.

Anthony is one of the most intense, hardworking, passionate, dedicated, knowledgeable, and committed hockey professionals that I know. His entire career in the strength and conditioning business has been built on 'the aggregation of marginal gains', constantly challenging himself to grow and to be better every single day. His insatiable thirst for scientific knowledge, the application of that knowledge, and the years he has spent at DSC (Donskov Strength and Conditioning, Columbus, OH) training hockey players and high performance athletes – have led him to the development of his book – **Physical Preparation for Ice Hockey.** Like everything Anthony does in his life – this book was built on passion – grit, work, integrity and love.

At its core – **Physical Preparation for Ice Hockey** is about the physiology of the game – energy systems, mobility, strength, acceleration, etc. Anthony explains in depth the integration of these component pieces creating a high performance model and strength and conditioning program for the novice and elite level ice hockey player. The book is organized into a logical, progressive format – taking you through the long-term athlete development model, assessment, preparation, bioenergetics, power training for hockey, and the principles of athletic based program design.

Physical Preparation for Ice Hockey is a practical, intuitive, user-friendly book for today's ice hockey strength and conditioning coach, high performance professional, manager, or hockey enthusiast – providing scientifically based process and protocol for athletic development programs and/or respective athletes.

I highly recommend this book for any strength coach, hockey professional, or hockey enthusiast seeking the knowledge of how to apply the very best scientifically researched athletic development principles to players, teams, and organizations.

Thanks Anth for your passion, knowledge, dedication, loyalty and energy. I am so fortunate to have a brother like you.

You make us all – One Day Better.

Love you bro.

Misha Donskov
Director of Hockey Operations
Vegas Golden Knights
National Hockey League

Preface

This book was written for both hockey player and coach. Hockey has been a passion of mine since early childhood. I was born and raised in Canada and relocated to the United States in 1990. Hockey has been the fabric of my family tree. From playing youth hockey to having the opportunity to play at the minor professional level, I have enjoyed this great game and the life lessons it has instilled along the way. It was during my career in university that coaching became a passion. I loved the weight room, the preparation, and the process. It was, and still is, a place of solace for me—a classroom. My love for strength and conditioning was born in the sweaty confines of the Miami (OH) University strength and conditioning facility located in Oxford, Ohio, and run by then strength and conditioning coach, Dan Dalrymple. Coach D. instilled pride, a strong work ethic, and belief in his athletes. Our two-thousand-square-foot weight room was a place of preparation and competition and embodied the team-first spirit. At that time, I knew my calling was to serve as a coach. I owe much gratitude and appreciation to Coach D. He was a mentor to me! Thanks, Coach. Your imprint has left an indelible mark.

My father was a coach. My older brother was a coach in the Ontario Hockey League and Manager of Hockey Operations/Analytics and Video for Hockey Canada and is a recent hire as director of hockey ops for the Vegas Golden Knights of the National Hockey League. My younger brother is also a coach. The word *coach* holds tremendous responsibility. We are responsible for not only physical development but the development of the *tangible intangibles*, such as work ethic, pride, commitment, attention to detail, desire, discipline, determination, and dedication. We are also responsible for instilling team spirit, sportsmanship, and love. Coaches have the ability to shape and alter lives. We must never take our positions for granted.

This book is a culmination of my experiences as both player and coach and serves as a guide for the practitioner to aid in designing the appropriate strength and conditioning protocol for hockey players. It is not a recipe book, checklist, or manual; it simply offers guidance and structure based on years of practical experience and sound science, which is subject to change on a continuous basis.

Many coaches have impacted my development, allowing me to build a solid foundation of pedagogy and practice. I could not do justice writing this book without acknowledging those who mentored, monitored, inspired, and challenged me to become the coach I am today. My father, who was my first hockey coach on the frozen ponds, always preached the *fun* in fundamentals; he was firm, yet fair and never judged success on scoreboard outcomes, goals, assists, or statistics but by development and work ethic. My brothers, both coaches and former players, have spent a lifetime growing this great game and shaping many lives along the way; they taught me patience and persistence. I must acknowledge their mentorship and love. We are, and will always be, pals! My first youth hockey coach Bill Scott, whose tireless commitment to bettering the lives of all he coached, will never be forgotten; he was transformational and made me become a better person. Coach Dan Dalrymple taught me to take pride in the details and fanned a flame of inspiration that still burns bright today. Coach Michael Boyle provided guidance and inspiration. Coach Sean Skahan took me under his wing and provided me with a unique opportunity to learn and apply, and Coach Chip Morton provided mentorship and guidance. There are many other coaches who have shaped my ideologies, and I am eternally thankful for their desire to share information via conversations, books, journals, articles, and DVDs. We are all on the same team, and although our methods may vary, our end goals are the same. Thank you all for shaping the path, for it is the journey that really matters.

Philosophy and Purpose

"Absorb. Modify. Apply." This is a quote I first heard from strength coach Joe Kenn and I try to live these words daily. I read incessantly, take notes, attend seminars, and try to get "one day better". This book is not an attempt to reinvent the wheel. I have learned from great coaches all of whom have had a major impact on my programming and how we, at DSC, train our respective populations. I hope I have done justice to all the coaches who have shaped my path.

In my professional career I have taken this acquired knowledge absorbed it, modified it (when necessary) to suit the resources, population, environment and applied it to enhance the results of our athletes. Our programs are subject to constant adaption, based on personal strengths/ weaknesses, theory and evolving scientific research.

It has been my purpose in writing this book to share how we absorb, modify and apply this information with our respective athletes.

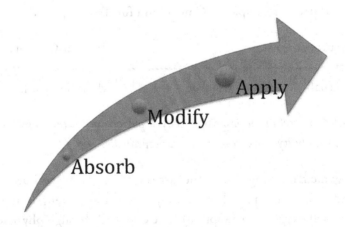

Apply

Modify

Absorb

Absorb:
Books
Seminars
Esteemed Coaches

Modify:
Resources
Population
Environment

Apply:
Clients
Athletes
Results

The Game

Hockey is a game of intermittent acceleration, speed, agility, strength, power, and capacity. Players can reach speeds of close to thirty miles per hour with an excess of twenty pounds of additional weight in the form of protective gear and padding. Shifts are kept short and contain 45 to 60 seconds of work characterized by short, two-second accelerations followed by coasting and decelerations of about 2.1 seconds.[1] In addition to skating at very high velocities, players can cover over five kilometers per game, depending on position.[2] Many defensemen are on the ice for approximately 50 percent of the game, compared to an average of 35 percent for forwards.[3] In order to meet these demands, the hockey player must harness multiple biomotor abilities that can tangibly be transferred onto the ice. A combination of power and the ability to consistently use that power, known as capacity, are both important components for the development of the athlete. Both are necessary to meet the demands of enhanced on-ice performance. Both are integral parts of the game.

Power and Capacity Continuum for Team Sports[4]

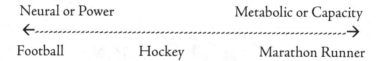

Neural or Power		Metabolic or Capacity
←	---	→
Football	Hockey	Marathon Runner

In order to excel in the game of hockey, a player must attain a high level of power and the ability to express this power repeatedly.

The game has changed over the last several years. Players are bigger, faster, and stronger than ever before. Body composition, strength, and VO2 max (maximal oxygen consumption) were obtained through physiological testing of Montreal Canadiens players between 1981 and 2003. Compared with players in the 1920s and 1930s, current players are an average of 17 kilograms heavier and 10 centimeters taller, with BMI increased by 2.3 kg/m².[5] Training camp is no longer the platform to attain peak playing condition. Failure to show up in shape may result in preventable injury and loss of playing time and ultimately may cost a player his or her job. Performance training is a forgone necessity. When the hour of performance arrives, the hour of preparation is over.

Improvement in on-ice ability requires much more than just playing hockey. Motor abilities, such as strength and power, are best developed off the ice. In other words, a player will not become stronger by playing more hockey. In order to properly prepare for the unique demands of the game, players must focus on a progressive, systemic program that incorporates soft-tissue work, movement economy, power, strength, and appropriate energy system training. In addition, these qualities need to be trained at different volumes and intensities, dependent on game schedule, time of year, needs analysis of each athlete, and current training readiness. This book takes a deeper look into these biological qualities and how to effectively structure a comprehensive program that addresses the athletes' needs while transferring these newfound gains onto the ice for increased performance.

Contents

Chapter 1

Long-Term Athletic Development (LTAD)

Most of the problems that exist in youth sports result from the inappropriate application of the win-oriented model of professional or elite sport to the child's sports setting.
—R.E. Smith (1984)

The difficulty lies not in the new ideas, but in escaping from the old ones.
—John Maynard Keynes

In the logical progression of motor acquisition and sequential learning, you must first learn to crawl before walking or attempting to run. Movement literacy serves as the foundation for technical and tactical application in higher-level sport. In order to perform at high levels, one must have a basic framework of motor competency. These building blocks provide the athlete with the appropriate foundation to further develop and become successful on the ice. Behind every complex skill lies a basic motor program. Hockey is not an early specialization sport. In order to develop the qualities needed to excel on the ice, players need to be exposed to multiple stimuli at early ages both on and off the ice.

Early Specialization	Late Specialization
▫ Routine based	▫ Highly technical
▫ Highly technical	▫ Decision-making efficiency
▫ Specific movement qualities	▫ Movement variability
▫ Sports: swimming, figure skating, and gymnastics	▫ Visual tracking
	▫ Sports: team sports

I, Balyi, R. Way, C. Higgs, *Long-Term Athletic Development*, (Human Kinetics, 2013).

Early specialization versus late specialization. Hockey is a late specialization sport.

1

The answer to enhanced skill development, including strength training, does not reside in playing more hockey games, specialized physical training, or placing adult values on childhood activities. The long-term athletic development (LTAD) model seeks to maximize athletic potential while sustaining passion and life-long love for sport.[6] Fundamental movement literacy is the bedrock for long-term athletic success in the sport of ice hockey. Furthermore, adult values, like the need to win at all costs, should never trump development and the early emergence of lifelong love for sport. This may compromise the learning process and lead to undesirable outcomes, such as burnout, chronic injury, and premature developmental issues.

Movement literacy, foundational human movement, such as kicking, jumping, throwing, receiving, catching, bounding, tumbling, and skipping, that serves as a foundational prerequisite for advanced activity.

The long-term athletic development model seeks to take advantage of biological training windows and introduce skills during the optimum point of physical development. The model, pioneered by sports scientist Istvan Balyi, creates a solid framework for young aspiring hockey players.

Long-term Athletic Development Model

The long-term athletic development model is used to maximize athletic potential and create lifelong physical activity.

Fundamentals

Ages Six to Nine

This is an important period when emotional ties to sport are developed. Fun is the name of the game. This is accomplished through small area games, multiple repetitions, and authentically learning skills through a trial-and-error process, without being overcoached or tied to rigid structural regimes. Children are encouraged to enjoy the game in adult-free play and learn through self-imposed cause-and-effect, trial-and-error experience. Agility, balance, coordination, and the first biological window for accelerated speed adaptation occur during this period. Speed adaptation is not *alactic* (highly neurological speed work consisting of six- to ten-second intervals coupled with adequate rest) in nature. In other words, it is not trained directly by engaging in pure speed training for an underdeveloped youth athlete. It is the reactive component of speed, which can be acquired by playing games that incorporate agility, change of direction, and quickness. This window occurs in females at approximately six to eight years of age and in males at approximately seven to nine.

3

Learn to Train (70/30 Percent Practice-to-Game Ratio)
Ages Nine to Twelve

This is a period where motor coordination can be introduced while the prior skills of the LTAD are maintained. Activities such as throwing, receiving, balance and basic unloaded patterning, such as squatting, hinging, pushing, and pulling can all be learned during this stage of physical maturation. A larger movement database allows the young athlete to reflexively respond to changing stimuli without hesitation and prelearned habits that may hinder response time. "If fundamental motor skill development is not developed between the ages of eight and eleven and nine and twelve for females and males, a significant window of opportunity has been lost."[7] Coaches may introduce a dynamic warm-up, focusing on movement economy, stability, and dynamic mobility. The focus still resides in playing multiple games and multiple sports while simultaneously increasing movement variability. Movement literacy is developed during the first two blocks of the athletic-based pyramid. It serves as the foundation of sport specificity and long-term participation. Failure to take advantage of these biological development windows compromises future development and may hinder long-term skill acquisition. During the final portions of this period, athletes will start to undergo changes in body composition and initiate puberty. As strength and conditioning professionals, it is wise to understand that weight training is not advised during this time.

Train-to-Train (60/40 Percent Practice to Game Ratio)
Ages Twelve to Sixteen

This period commences with an increase in anabolic hormone profiles, including testosterone and growth hormone. During this window, structured strength training and conditioning may take place. Aerobic exercise may also be introduced. The cardiorespiratory system is now prepared for greater demands, as growth of both the heart and lungs accelerates and blood volume expands. "Optimal aerobic trainability begins with the onset of peak height velocity. According to Hollmann, the greatest increase in heart volume occurs at approximately eleven years of age for girls, and approximately fourteen years of age for boys."[8] Special emphasis is also required for flexibility training because of the sudden growth of bones and this effect on tendons, ligaments, and muscles. Many times, the skeletal system grows at an accelerated rate compared with soft tissue. This may place certain soft tissue structures in tight, facilitated states. During this period, players can select a late-specialization sport. This should typically occur between the ages of twelve and fifteen. It is wise to choose one winter sport and one summer sport with noncompeting schedules. This allows the athlete to further refine biomotor skills without schedule conflict. From the experience of the author, the later this decision can be made, the better.

Train to Compete (40/60 Percent Practice-to-Game Ratio)
Ages Sixteen to Eighteen

The focus now shifts from general to specific in terms of development. Periodization and position-specific training should be introduced as such structured ebbs and flows in the training process begin to take shape. Periodization simply means training in periods and provides the coach with structure, dividing the annual plan into transition, preparation, and competition blocks, each block representing various dates within the annual plan. Without a foundation of physical literacy, specificity may become compromised, as poor skill development may expose the athlete to inefficient and compromised performance.

Train to Win (25/75 Percent Practice-to-Game Ratio)
Ages Eighteen and Older

This period seeks to maximize all performance abilities. Physical preparation, psychological preparation, and technical and tactical abilities are all coached on a solid platform of retained biomotor abilities. Practice-to-game ratio is noticeably reduced, providing the athlete more time to focus on his or her specific skill set.

Active for Life

There is a better opportunity to be active for life if physical literacy is achieved before the training-to-train stage. Playing multiple sports at an early age enhances the probability of an athlete developing a lifelong love for physical activity.

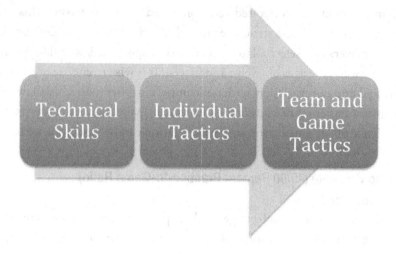

(Slide courtesy of www.donskovhockey.com.) Technical skills, such as skating, shooting, puck handling, and passing are paramount in the development process of the hockey player. In order for a player to use individual and team tactics, fundamental technical skills must exist—the more skill, the more variability of specific tactics. The same rationale holds true when focusing on off-ice athletic preparation.

Factors Influencing the Model
Ten Factors Influencing the LTAD Model
1. The ten-year rule
2. Fundamentals
3. Specialization
4. Developmental age
5. Trainability
6. Physical, mental, cognitive, and emotional development
7. Periodization
8. Calendar planning
9. System alignment and integration
10. Continuous improvement

Ten Thousand Hours
There are ten factors that influence the model and its ability to impact motor competency. For the sake of brevity, the author will discuss two such factors. One of the major factors influencing the LTAD model is the

ten-thousand-hour rule.[9] Research has shown that it takes ten thousand hours of deliberate practice to reach the pinnacle of any profession. For a player, or a coach, this translates into three hours each day of practice for ten years. This is the time needed to harness physiological, psychological, and neurological development. The base of this development is anchored by physical literacy. The structure of a pyramid is only as strong as its foundation. Without a strong, structural base, implosion will result. This can be in the form of poor skill levels, burnout, chronic injury, and an eventual loss of passion for the game. You can't shoot a cannon out of a canoe. The process of building strong, powerful hockey players cannot be attained without first building appropriate requisite skills; playing more games does not accomplish this goal. Skill acquisition is accumulated through constant repetition, deliberate practice and the appropriate use of free time.

> In a study done by former NHL Coach George Kingston in 1976 he found that the average player in the Canadian system spent 17.6 minutes on the ice during a typical game and was in possession of the puck for an astonishingly low 41 seconds. Kingston concluded that in order to get one hour of quality work in the practicing of the basic skills of puck control, (that is, stick-handling, passing, pass receiving and shooting) approximately 180 games would have to be played.[10]

More games = < skill development, < skill development = < fun, < fun = < participation, < participation = > sedentary youth

In the construction of ten thousand hours, deliberate practice, small area games, free time, and early exposure to varying sporting demands are all more important than the games themselves or the outcomes of the games. Games should be adapted to fit the skill level of the athlete where basic skills, multiple puck touches, quick decision making, and skating mechanics can be challenged in a tight, confined, fun environment. It is during these formative years that the pillars of athletic achievement are harnessed. In addition, the ten-thousand-hour rule seeks to exploit motor efficiency by creating unconscious competence, whereby the athlete

7

performs with precision and accuracy in response to changing conditions on the ice without conscious thought.

The Four Stages of Learning a New Skill

Unconscious Incompetence	Mistakes are made unconsciously.
Conscious Incompetence	By repetitive repetition and coaching, the athlete recognizes these inefficiencies.
Conscious Competence	Proper skill is executed with thought and effort.
Unconscious Competence	Proper skill is executed effortlessly without thought.

The goal of motor acquisition is to respond to a change in stimulus with a plethora of movement-based options. The more options the nervous system possesses, the more choices it has in reaching the appropriate response efficiently.

At an early age (birth to twelve years), exposure to a variety of movement is paramount. Kicking, running, jumping, throwing, tumbling, catching, receiving, decelerating, changing direction, skipping, hopping, maintaining balance, and refining motor coordination are a few of the activities that can be introduced early through small area games, playing multiple sports, and the adequate use of unsupervised free time. This period also sets the stage for developing the requisites required to initiate strength and conditioning protocol during the train-to-train period. If the athlete is unprepared physically when he or she reaches this biological period, progress will be stalled and development compromised.

Adapt the sport to the athlete, not the athlete to the sport.
—Anthony Donskov

It is during the early stages of athletic development when free time and multiple exposures to various sports establish a large database of movement literacy. The larger the database, the more options may be utilized during the demands of sport where decisions are not memorized and creative response leads to superior performance outcomes. Ken Dryden sums it up quite eloquently:

> It is in free time that the special player develops, not in the competitive expedience of games, in hour-long practices once a week, in mechanical devotion to packaged, processed, coaching-manual, hockey-school skills. For while skills are necessary, setting out as they do the limits of anything, more is needed to transform those skills into something special. Mostly it is time unencumbered, unhurried, time of a different quality, more time, time to find wrong answers to find a few that are right; time to find your own right answers; time for skills to be practiced to set higher limits, to settle and assimilate and become fully and completely yours, to organize and combine with other skills comfortably and easily in some uniquely personal way, then to be set loose, trusted, to find new instinctive directions to take, to create.
>
> But without such time a player is like a student cramming for exams. His skills are like answers memorized by his body, specific, limited to what is expected, random and separate, with no overviews to organize and bring them together. And for those times when more is demanded, when new unexpected circumstances come up, when answers are asked for things you've never learned, when you must intuit and piece together what you already know to find new answers, memorizing isn't enough. It's the difference between knowledge and understanding, between a super-achiever and a wise old man. And it's the difference between a modern suburban player and a player like Lafleur. (Ken Dryden's CBC-TV series, *Home Game*)

Trainability Windows

Another major factor influencing this model is the idea of biological training windows, or sensitive periods in athletic development. "The sensitive periods are periods in human life when the organs and systems that determine a given ability are under development."[11]

"Developmental age refers to the degree of physical, mental, cognitive, and emotional maturity. Physical developmental age can be determined by skeletal maturity or bone age after which mental, cognitive, and emotional maturity is incorporated."[12]

As we can see in the LTAD pyramid, *fundamental* basic skills, such as agility, balance, and coordination can be provided at an early age (six to nine years) through the use of fun and games. This can take place after practice or during the summer months. Basic motor coordination can be attacked during the learn-to-train block. This is a window of opportunity to introduce a dynamic warm-up or games focusing on quickness and change of direction. It is only after the development of balance, agility, and basic motor coordination that the strength and conditioning practitioner may safely address basic strength, suppleness, and stamina without compromise.

Development of the Five Ss

Speed	Fundamentals Early window: females 6–8, males 7–9 Learn to train Late window: females 11–13, males 13–16 agility, balance, coordination
Skill	Learn to train
Suppleness	Learn to train, train to train
Stamina	Train to train and beyond
Strength	Train to train and beyond

The bottom line is that hockey players need a variety of unsupervised exposures in ever-changing learning environments without early specialization or preprogrammed sport-specific drills that focus on the outcome (winning) rather than the process. Winning should not be stressed. The early years of an athlete's career are when passion, love, and emotional ties are set for lifelong love of sport. The weight room is a highly structured, preprogrammed environment of controlled stress application. Prior to commencement of the weight room, a solid level of physical literacy is paramount.

Final Thoughts on Long-Term Athletic Development

+ Athletes learn from trial and error. It is important that during development the athlete be exposed to a variety of experiences. Hockey is *not* an early specialization sport.

+ Early specialization limits motor variability and restricts motor learning. Too much specialized focus may lead to preprogramed responses to changing conditions on the ice. In addition, structured time and prepackaged drills in controlled environments inhibit creativity and natural development.

+ The greater the database, the more efficient the nervous system.

+ Always seek to expand the database.

+ Excellence takes time.

+ Umbrella theory states that a person with a large surface area umbrella of protection made of mobility, stability, and strength is able to move freely under the umbrella without getting wet.[13] Focusing on the basics can prevent long-term chronic injury and set out to make the sporting experience fun and rewarding.

+ Long-term athletic development increases motor efficiency. Efficiency is output relative to the cost of input.

+ Limitations in movement mean limitations in sport.

+ Young athletes are *not* miniature adults.

+ Strength and conditioning should be based on biological readiness. If you do not understand basic mathematics (physical literacy), you cannot perform advanced algebra (weight training).

+ Players may select a late-specialization sport when they are between the ages of twelve and fifteen—the later the better.

+ Structured strength and conditioning for ice hockey should begin between the ages of twelve and fourteen.

+ Do not dream on behalf of your child.

- The more complicated the skill, the more heavily the athlete relies upon previously learned skills and abilities.
- Redefine performance metrics. Don't keep score during early childhood development.
  - Redefine wining. Focus on improvement and skill development.
  - Fill emotional tanks by being positive and providing mentorship.
  - Honor the game, the rules, the officials, and your teammates. Sport is an extension of life.
- Have *fun*! Embrace the journey.

Chapter 2

Assessment

The aim of athletic training should be to enable the individual
to tolerate training loads and therefore maximize his or
her exposure to technical and tactical coaching.
—David Joyce and Daniel Lewindon

In order to safely and effectively tolerate a prescribed training load, a basic fitness assessment is necessary. Assessing both the movement and fitness qualities of the athlete aids the coach in providing a program specific to the athlete's direct needs, individual orthopedic structure, previous injury history, and sporting demands. The assessment gives the coach an opportunity to gauge static posture, dynamic movement, and any potential asymmetries prior to load being placed on the athlete. This is of utmost importance for hockey players, as mobility, stability, and overall strength levels directly influence skating mechanics, in particular, stride length. The end goal is to build a balanced athlete while directly evaluating physiological needs and motor qualities that may be lacking. This balance serves as a solid foundation for the hockey player to further build appropriate levels of sport-specific technical and tactical skills.

The Balanced Athlete

> **Functional Skill**

> **Functional Performance/General Fitness**

> **Functional Movement**

From Gray Cook's Athletic Body in Balance,[14] *the balanced athlete possesses a solid foundation of movement. This enables the coach to build adequate levels of general and specific fitness, coupled with the skill demands (technical and tactical) of hockey.*

The Underpowered Athlete

> **Functional Skill**

> **Functional Performance/General Fitness**

> **Functional Movement**

The underpowered athlete has a solid base of movement proficiency but lacks fundamental motor abilities, such as strength, power, and strength endurance.[15]

The Overpowered Athlete

Functional Skill

Functional Performance/General Fitness

Functional Movement

The overpowered athlete lacks a solid foundation of movement proficiency and many times attempts to build strength over dysfunction. This can lead to mechanical inefficiency on the ice as well as increased potential for chronic injury during the course of the hockey season.[16]

A basic assessment may be broken down into the following categories:

Subjective Information
- Health history
- Needs analysis

Postural/Movement-Based Tests
- Static posture
- Table assessments
- FMS

Fitness-Based Tests
- Strength testing
- Alactic
- Lactic
- Aerobic

Subjective Information

A basic health history questionnaire is extremely important to the practitioner prior to the commencement of any exercise demands upon the circulatory system. Each athlete should be medically cleared in order to participate in a comprehensive strength and conditioning program. Of particular importance to the hockey player is the heart. Hypertrophic cardiomyopathy (HCM) is a genetic disease that causes the walls of the left ventricle to thicken and not to relax completely between beats, which can impede blood flow into the heart itself. HCM is the most common cause of natural sudden death in young people. Cardiac assessment by a medical professional is vital prior to the introduction of exercise-related stressors, which create a direct stimulus on the circulatory system. The following is a basic health history questionnaire that has been used in the private sector at Donskov Strength and Conditioning. It is designed for ease of use and generally takes five to ten minutes for the athlete to complete.

***

Health History

Please answer yes or no as to whether any of the following pertains to you. If you answer "yes," please explain in the space provided.

Y/N Initials

1. Heart problems: _____

_____

2. High blood pressure: _____

_____

3. Respiratory problems: _____

_____

4. Diabetes: _____

_____

5. Surgery: _____

_____

6. Hospitalization: _____

_____

7. Muscle, joint, or spine-related injury: _____

_____

Treatment/Status: _____

_____

8. Medication: _____

_____

9. Nonprescription Supplements: _____

_____

10. Smoker: _____

_____

11. Alcoholic beverages: _____

_____

12. Are you currently on an exercise program: _____

_____

13. How would you rate your current state of health: _____

_____

14. Medical approval for exercise: _____

_____

Personal Information

Top Three Personal Health and Fitness Goals

1. _____

_____

2. _____

_____

3. _____

_____

How many days per week can you realistically devote to exercise? ____

_____

How many days per week would you like to train with me? _____

_____

Name: _____ Phone: _____

Address: _____ Work: _____

City/State/Zip: _____ Mobile: _____

Email: _____

***

Needs Analysis

What are the qualities needed to become an effective, efficient hockey player? These are the questions answered in a basic needs analysis. The needs analysis provides the coach insight regarding appropriate fitness testing that directly correlates to on-ice performance while developing bigger, faster, and stronger hockey players. The needs analysis serves as a blueprint for program design, testing, and retesting and provides a measuring stick for assessing program results.

Needs Analysis

- **Movement Impairments/Previous Injury**
  Does the player have a current injury, previous surgery, and/or chronic musculotendinous
  Issue that may impede performance or directly affect program design?

- **What are the qualities needed to be a successful Hockey Player?**
  Hockey is an important team sport requiring acceleration, COD, transition, strength, speed,
  power and capacity. The player must be able to sustain power output relative to the coarse of a 60-
  minute hockey game pending position, overall ice time and certain on-ice situations
  (PP, PK, Overtime).

- **What kind of a player are you?**
  A power forward? A skilled finesse player? A player who needs to watch his/her body comp?
  A player prone to injury?

- **What type of player does your Coach want you to become?**
  What does your Coach think you need to improve upon? Acceleration, overall game
  Conditioning, strength, power, mental toughness, first step starting strength?

- **What are the energy system demands of the sport? Work: Rest Ratio.**
  Ice hockey is characterized by high intensity, short-duration sprints (2).
  There is a demand on both aerobic and anaerobic energy systems which
  most intermittent sports require. The work to rest ration may vary from 1:5 – 1:1
  pending position, game situation and allotted ice time.

- **Positional demands? Defense? Forward? Goalie?**
  What are the positional demands? This may affect energy system training depending on the
  neural or metabolic demands of the position. Certainly positions on the ice warrant both aerobic and
  anaerobic contribution, but at different ratios and capacities.

  Power/Capacities continuum for positional play in Ice Hockey.

- **Common injuries associated with Ice Hockey**
  Hockey currently has the highest incidence of athlete-to-athlete trauma in
  sport. The percentage of injuries that occur during games is 13.5% knee
  injuries, 8.9% acromioclavicular (AC) joint injuries, 6.2% upper leg contusions and
  4.5% pelvis and hip muscle strains.

Basic Needs Analysis for Hockey Players

Posture/Movement-Based Tests

Movement first, volume second, load third.
—Dan John

In order to properly view the athlete in various planes, it is recommended
that images be taken in the sagittal plane (facing and behind the athlete)
and in the frontal plane (from the side of the athlete). It is also wise to view

the athlete in a single leg posture to assess how the body compensates and stabilizes in unilateral stance. Although these tests only offer subjective information, gross asymmetries or postural guarding (the nervous systems inability to turn down efferent input to the over active muscle) may also be identified and further magnified by the practitioner during the movement-based follow-up.

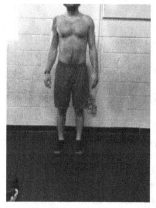  

1   2   3

(1) Sagittal plane view: notice right leg stance with lower right shoulder/hand. This athlete may have a malpositioned left innominate, while stuck in contralateral right side internal rotation/extension. Position equals power!

(2) Posterior view: notice the right interior boarder of the scapula is depressed and lower than the left. Right ribs are stuck in internal rotation.

(3) Frontal plane static assessment: anterior weight displacement, which may be due to a bilateral anterior pelvic tilt.

Hockey is played in a flexed hip position, placing both concentric and isometric stress on the hips and quadriceps during long duration force application. The specificity of this mechanical position places a specific postural adaptation on the player, facilitating certain muscle synergists while inhibiting or turning off others. Basic static imaging may reveal these potential imbalances.

The result of this stress can result in both upper-crossed and lower-crossed syndrome as referred to by Dr. Vladimir Janda.

Upper-Crossed Syndrome

- Weak or inhibited deep neck flexors, lower traps, and serratus.
- Tight or facilitated pectorals, upper traps, and levator scapula.
- The result of these imbalances may lead to a malposition of the cervical spine and thorax, which may affect respiration via facilitated anterior scalenes and SCM, not permitting the diaphragm to work efficiently and effectively as a muscle of respiration. The accessory muscles take over and *neck breathing* is the result. In addition, the thoracic spine and scapula become compromised. The position of the thorax dictates the position and function of the scapula. This places the shoulder in an internally rotated position and anteriorly tips the scapula, exposing the hockey player to impingement and increasing the potential for an impact injury to this anatomical landmark.

Lower-Crossed Syndrome

- Weak or inhibited gluteus maximus and anterior core.
- Tight or facilitated hip flexors and erector spinae.
- The result of these imbalances may lead to a malpositioned pelvis. An anteriorly tipped pelvis places the glutes in an inhibited position via reciprocal inhibition of the tight facilitated hip flexors. This simply means the glutes cannot fire appropriately, which places excessive demands elsewhere in the system. In addition to tight hip flexors, tight erector spinae can inhibit the anterior core. This can result in a tug-of-war between tight, facilitated hip flexors and a weak, inhibited midsection, in particular the rectus abdominus. The lack of adjacent core stiffness may result in sports hernias and other chronic hip issues associated with the demands of the game. Osteitis pubis and femoacetabular hip impingement (FAI) are growing concerns among the hockey-playing population. It is currently unclear whether this repetitive stress and recurrent activity on the hips leads to the structural changes associated with FAI. However, the vulnerable positions of flexion, internal rotation and abduction associated with the hockey

stride may be more prone to breakdown under a malpositioned, nonneutral pelvis. Any machine operating in compromised position, including the human body, leads to decreased efficiency, increased fuel demand, and an increase in chronic overload. Power equals position!

Another pattern that the practitioner may see in the athlete during static assessment is the left anterior interior chain (AIC) or a posterior exterior chain (PEC) pattern. Although a detailed description of these patterns is beyond the scope of this book, further information on these imbalances may be found through the Postural Restoration Institute (www.posturalrestoration.com). The basis for these underlying movement patterns lies in functional anatomy and the fact that our bodies are not designed for neutrality. As humans, our thorax, along with vital organs, is different from right to left. This affects our alignment and may cause us to use our fuel (a.k.a. oxygen) inefficiently. The body will always choose survival over positioning, which may lead to faulty breathing patterns and compromised performance.

Right Versus Left

- There are three lobes of lung on the right and two on the left.
- The liver is on the right.
- There is a bigger central tendon and pull from the right diaphragm versus the left.
- The right diaphragm is higher in orientation.
- The right crus of the diaphragm arises from the bodies of the first three lumbar vertebrae and their intervertebral discs. The left crus arises from the bodies of the first two lumbar vertebrae. This affects leverage.

These anatomical right versus left differences that all humans have can place us into faulty patterns that affect daily respiration and movement.

Left AIC

- Malpositioned pelvis
- Anteriorly tipped left hemipelvis in position of abduction, external rotation, and flexion, with an increase in left hamstring length

- Posteriorly tipped right hemipelvis in position of adduction, internal rotation, and extension
- Increased rib flare on the left with difficulty rotating to the right

PEC

- Bilateral anterior tilt of pelvis
- Lower body positioned in abduction, flexion, and external rotation
- Stiff thoracic spine stuck in extension

Table Assessments

Table assessments work in conjunction with static posture in digging deeper into any potential compensatory imbalances an athlete may have acquired. There are a plethora of table assessments that the coach may use to further assess the athlete. Decisions on testing protocol should be based on the following:

- Demands of the sport
- Biomechanics of the sport
- Tools of the trade (i.e., anatomical areas of importance)
- Previous injury history

Adduction Drop Test/Ober's Test

Positioning is crucial in economizing efficiency and enhancing power output. Lack of positioning may lead to energy leaks and chronic injury. Is the hockey player in a position of neutrality? This table test seeks to provide the coach with a baseline of pelvic position. The hockey player lies on the table in a side-lying position with the hips and knees flexed at a ninety-degree angle. The coach then abducts the leg being tested and allows gravity to adduct the extremity to end range. If the player cannot adduct past midline or if the player falls into excessive extension, the test is deemed positive. This can be due to an anteriorly tipped left innominate or bilateral pelvic position stemming from the excessive demand on the hip flexors engaged in prolonged static posture from the skating position.

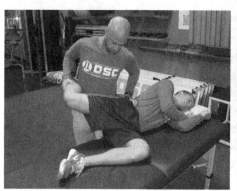

Adduction Drop Test

Craig's Test

This test is designed to assess femoral version. The normal angulation of the neck of the femur relative to femoral condyles is five to fifteen degrees. If the hockey player exhibits femoral anteverion (greater than fifteen-degree angle), he or she will be required to internally rotate in order to allow the head of the femur to be properly positioned in the hip (acetabulum). Conversely, if this angle is less than five degrees (retroversion), the hockey player will be required to externally rotate in order to allow the head of the femur to be properly positioned in the acetabulum. This has implications for exercise design and may require the omission of certain exercises based on the player's orthopedics. For example, anteverted hips perfrom better with flexion, but are compromised during extension. Retroverted hips may be compromised during flexion, while they perfrom better during extension. Exercises should be chosen accordingly. The end range in a squat pattern is achieved faster for certain populations based on bony anatomy. For example retroverted hips may limit squat depth. Deep flexion coupled with internal rotation may cause the head of the femur to impinge on the acetabulum, creating friction and resulting in chronic pain. Attacking core stiffness and the posterior chain are much better alternatives.

To perform Craig's test, the athlete lies facedown on the table while the coach palpates the greater trochanter. The coach passively internally and externally rotates the thigh and measures where the greater trochanter is in its most lateral position. If the tibia is rotated outward more than fifteen degrees, anteverion is the result. If the tibia is rotated less than five degrees, retroversion is the result. Although these tests may be subjective, based on the technique used by the practitioner, they do provide baseline information that may aid in program design and individualization based on orthopedics.

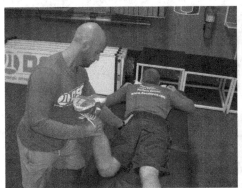

Craig's Test

Thomas Test

The player sits on the edge of the table and gently falls backward, lying supine with both knees flexed into the midsection. The coach gently places one hand under the athlete to make sure the lower back is flush to the table. The coach then uses his or her other hand and guides the tested limb passively until end range. The test is deemed positive if the athlete cannot reach the table with the tested leg. This test has traditionally been used to assess hip flexor length, but it's important to appreciate that pelvic positioning will have a direct impact on test results. If the hockey player's hips are anteriorly tipped bilaterally or unilaterally, it can place the psoas on slack and potentially give the coach a false positive as the femur butts up against the lip of the acetabulum. Therefore, alignment dictates mobility, stability, and length tension differences around the joint.

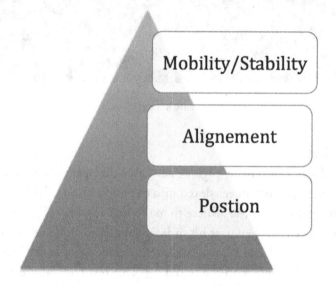

Position dictates alignment. Alignment dictates mobility and stability. Mobility and stability dictate functional movement.

Dynamic Assessment: Functional Movement Screen

The functional movement screen serves as a dynamic assessment prior to loading the athlete. This screen allows the practitioner to view authentic movement in a controlled environment and aids in decision-making, regarding program-based progressions and regressions. This tool essentially assesses risk. If an athlete cannot complete a pattern efficiently, pain free and unloaded, why would a coach want to load the pattern and potentially increase the chance of injury? The creator of the screen,

Gray Cook, eloquently states, "We should not put fitness on movement dysfunction." Can the hockey player perform the movement pain free? Are there any compensations exhibited while he or she is attempting to perform the desired pattern? Can the hockey player perform the movement efficiently and effectively?

Scoring the FMS

0.) Pain: Coach refers the athlete to the appropriate medical authority prior to program initiation.
1.) The athlete cannot perform the required movement. Pain is not the limiting factor. Faulty mobility or stability may be the cause.
2.) The athlete can perform the movement but has several compensations in completing it.
3.) The athlete proficiently performs the movement with efficiency and required technique.

Functional Movement Screen: how to score each individual movement

For more information regarding the FMS, scoring the FMS, and its application and use, the reader is urged to visit: http://www.functionalmovement.com/. The following is the FMS scoring sheet used in the private sector at Donskov Strength and Conditioning.

DONSKOV
Strength and Conditioning, Inc.

Functional Movement Screen

Name: _____ Date: _____

Height: _____ Weight: _____ Age: _____

Sport: _____ Position: _____

Hand/Leg Dominance: _____ Previous Score: _____

Tibia Measurement: _____ Hand Measurement: _____

Test	Raw Score	Final Score	Comments
Deep Squat			
Hurdle Step	L _____ R		
In-Line Lunge	L _____ R		
Shoulder Mobility	L _____ R		
Active Straight Leg Raise	L _____ R		
Trunk Stability Push-Up			
Rotary Stability	L _____ R		

Totals _____ _____ _____

Raw Score—This score denotes right and left scoring.

Final Score—This score is the overall score of the test. The lowest score for the raw score is carried over to formulate a final score for the movement.

There have been several studies[17] using diagnostic statistics that establish a low score cutoff of less than 14. Any test scored below this threshold may be a predictor of increased injury. It bears repeating that everything in the weight room can be used as an assessment—movement, foot contacts during jump training, athlete demeanor, overall subjective stress scores, athlete readiness technology, and a plethora of other tools. The FMS simply provides a snapshot of seven basic human movement patterns and prevents the practitioner from potentially loading a pattern that may be compromising and possibly dangerous.

Movement Screen Observations from the Hockey-Playing Population

- **Poor ankle mobility**—Inadequate ankle dorsiflexion (dorsiflexion is the ability to extend the toes and ankle joint toward the ceiling) can be seen during the OH squat and in-line lunge tests. Skate boots are extremely stiff and during basic striding patterns offer minimal room for movement within the ankle complex. Poor ankle dorsiflexion can lead to knee problems, energy leaks, and poor stride mechanics. Weak knee bend may lead to decrease in stride length and poor balance on the ice. Essentially the hockey player's center of gravity is affected by limited dorsiflexion placing the center of mass too far forward in front of the player. This causes instability and faulty stride mechanics and does not allow the player to utilize the powerful stretch reflex in the Achilles tendon affectively. If this reflex is not fully exploited, power loss is the direct result.

- **Poor shoulder mobility**—Poor shoulder mobility is commonplace in the hockey-playing population. This is directly assessed with the shoulder mobility breakout in the FMS. This issue may be caused by sitting for prolonged periods of time throughout the day, technological advancements (such as the computer and mobile phone), or poor training habits with an overemphasis on pushing protocol. Poor shoulder mobility may also be the by-product of exaggerated kyphosis acquired from faulty positioning on the ice.

Many hockey players struggle with adequate shoulder mobility. This places the shoulder joint in an excessive internally rotated and adducted position. The scapula also shifts leverage into an anteriorly tipped forward position. The position of the thorax affects scapular positioning, and scapular positioning, in turn, affects the glenohumeral joint and the surrounding length tension of the rotator cuff group.

- **Hip flexor impairment**—This pattern can be viewed during the hurdle step. If the player fails to keep the hips neutral during single leg stance, it may be an issue of impaired hip flexion. This may be due to synergistic dominance of the TFL and rectus femoris. These muscles may compensate because of the inhibition of the psoas and illacus respectively. Hip flexor impairment may lead to soft-tissue injuries around the anterior hip and decrease impulse during the hockey stride.

A person with a large surface area umbrella of protection
made of mobility, stability, and strength is able to move
freely under the umbrella without getting wet.
—Darcy Norman

Additional Test: Ankle Dorsiflexion

Hockey is played in skates. The mold, stiffness, and tightness of both the boot and laces can affect ankle dorsiflexion. Inadequate dorsiflexion can affect stride length and center of gravity and lead to unwanted energy leaks and accumulated fatigue.

This is a pass/fail test. The practitioner places measuring tape five inches from the wall. The athlete assumes a half-kneeling position (some coaches prefer a standing position) with the lead toe in line with the start of the tape measure. The athlete then attempts to touch his or her knee to the wall without allowing the heel of the tested foot to rise. Knee drive is toward the fifth (baby) toe.

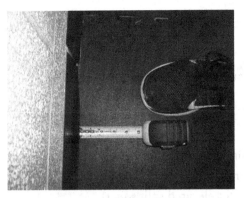 

Fitness-Based Testing

> If it will not influence the program or the athlete, don't test it.
> —Doug Kechijian

Fitness-based testing serves to bridge the gap between movement capacity and athletic performance. Fitness testing can aid the strength coach in assessing physical talent, identifying motor abilities that need direct improvement, and recording the progress of the athlete throughout the duration of his or her career in the weight room. Review of the needs analysis can provide the coach with valid information and insight that has direct influence on the particulars of testing protocol. The abilities tested are based on the demands of the game and the qualities needed to perform at maximal levels on the ice. It should be noted that the young, inexperienced athlete with minimal training age and experience should not be loaded during testing as he or she may not be able to perform basic unloaded patterns safely and effectively. Safety is the number-one consideration for the coach, and he or she needs to consider the training age. In order for testing to be considered by the coaching staff, it must be both valid (test what it sets out to test) and reliable (repeatable). The following are several tests that can be used to assess the fitness levels of the competitive hockey player.

- **Alactic Tests**—Alactic testing measures power output and the ability of the ATP-PC (adenosine triphosphate phosphocreatine) system to produce force within a minimal time frame (less than ten seconds).

- □ Vertical jump
- □ Ten-meter sprint
- □ Broad jump
- □ Lateral bound (test both left and right)
- □ 5 RM strength testing
  - ○ Upper body: bench press or push-ups for time (less than ten seconds)
  - ○ Upper body: chin-ups or chin-ups for time (less than ten seconds)
  - ○ Lower body: back squat / front squat
  - ○ Lower body: RFESS (rear foot elevated split squat)

- ♦ **Lactic Tests**—Lactic testing measures the ability to generate power output under conditions close to and beyond lactic acid critical levels (16 to 18mM/l) during glycolysis. This typically takes place within a 30- to 120-second time window.
- □ Three-hundred-yard repeat shuttle—Cones are placed 25 yards apart (Coaches may also opt for a 50-yard distance). On the coach's verbal cue, the athlete runs back and forth six times, performing the required three hundred yards. Upon completion, a three- to five-minute rest interval is granted prior to the athlete performing the test for the second time. Coaches should time each shuttle and compare the difference between the two times. This is called the *drop off*. Drop off indicates the athlete's ability to recover and perform the test again without significant performance decrements. Coaches should look for no more than a 3 second drop off between each shuttle.

  This test is a lactic endeavor characterized by relatively low power outputs. It does not bare much relation to the bioenergetic structure of most team sports (alactic-aerobic), including hockey. It is rare to see an elite player skate full speed during the course of a 45-to-60-second shift. Coaches should take this into consideration prior to testing.

- ♦ **Aerobic Tests**—These tests measure the ability to generate sustainable power output for a prolonged duration. The time frame used for aerobic conditioning tests may be as short as two minutes for aerobic power and as long as several hours for aerobic capacity.

▫ Modified Cooper's (use a heart rate monitor)—This test can be performed on a bike or on a track. The athlete bikes or runs for six minutes while sustaining maximal power output. The coach tracks total distance covered; maximum heart rate upon completion, anaerobic threshold (this is calculated as the average heart rate during each minute of the six minute test), and one-minute heart rate recovery. This test places emphasis on aerobic capacity, which is vital for recovery between bouts of maximal efforts on the ice.

▫ Multistage beep test—This test is a progressive aerobic endurance test that seeks to estimate an athlete's VO2Max. Place two cones twenty meters apart. The athlete's performs a series of shuttles on the beep. If the athlete fails to reach the other side before the beep, the test is deemed over.

♦ **Mixed Tests (Alactic/Aerobic)**

▫ Repeat sprint ability—Repeat sprint ability is characterized by short-duration sprints (less than ten seconds) interspersed with brief recovery periods (usually less than sixty seconds). Anaerobic glycolysis supplies approximately 40 percent of the total energy during a single six-second sprint, but this number shifts toward aerobic contribution as the number of sprints increase.[18]

The coach places two cones twenty meters (sixty-five feet) apart. The athlete performs ten total sprints every thirty seconds. The coach documents best time, average time, and the fatigue index. The fatigue index for running is calculated as follows:

$$FI \text{ (running)} = 100 \times \frac{S \text{ slowest} - S \text{ fastest}}{S \text{ fastest}}[31]$$

By no means are these the only significant off-ice testing protocols; however, they are effective in measuring the appropriate motor abilities and energy systems needed to be efficient and effective on the ice. After completing the health history, needs analysis, and static/

dynamic assessments, the coach will have obtained important physical assessments and have a better idea of developing a training plan based on the following:

- Chronological age
- Training age
- Competition demands
- Short-term goals
- Long-term goals
- Physiological limitations
- Movement limitations
- Athlete's personality
- Stressors of the nontraining environment

The end goal of the assessment process is to build a blueprint, an athlete-centric program, which prepares the athlete to perform at top levels of the sport. Furthermore, the assessment process focuses on addressing areas of weakness while reinforcing areas of strength—maximizing potential while economizing time. If the practitioner is working in a team setting, testing results should be presented to the coaching staff within seventy-two hours. This time frame offers the strength coach adequate opportunity to document, analyze, and provide the coaching staff with time-sensitive results. These results may affect team dynamics, roster placement, and practice planning. As the sports practitioner meets with the coaching staff and shares the assessment and testing results, he or she assists in promoting staff cohesion and building an interdisciplinary approach, which validates and solidifies the importance of building an athlete-first system.

Chapter 3

Preparation

> When learning to cook the new dish from the recipe, an inexpert
> cook catches mostly the quantity of the ingredients, an expert
> cook—rather the way and the sequence of their addition.
> —Yuri Verkoshansky

In order to prepare the body for the demands of increased effort, an appropriate warm-up is necessary. A comprehensive warm-up serves to accomplish the following:

- Decrease tissue density
- Increase circulation
- Increase ROM and amplitude
- Increase movement economy
- Increase muscle temperature
- Increase temperature (hemoglobin gives away more oxygen at higher temperatures)
- Enhance gas exchange
- Increase muscle pliability
- Increase motor coordination
- Increase mental focus
- Reinforce neuromuscular patterning used under load

The warm-up is sequenced, using appropriate progressions. Progressions enable the athlete to challenge the neuromuscular system, using basic transitions from simple to complex, slow to fast, closed loop to open loop, and so on. In addition, the sequence is constructed with the idea of favorable prerequisites. This means that a deliberate order is constructed so that each modality feeds off the method that precedes it. This provides structure, balance, and favorable circumstances for motor preparation.

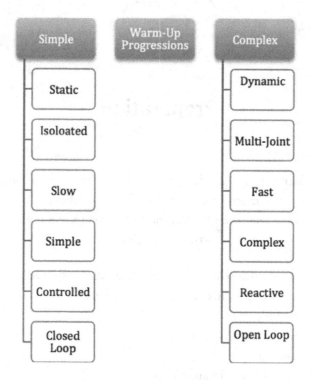

Table 3.1 Warm-Up Progressions

Foam Rolling

Tissue Density

Foam rolling serves to increase circulation, decrease tissue density, and prepare the muscle for activity. This is accomplished through the process called *autogenic inhibition*. As the foam roller applies pressure to the muscle tissue; mechanoreceptors called Golgi tendon organs (located in the musculotendinous junction) send a message to the brain that considerable tension is being placed on the muscle, and the brain responds by causing the muscle to relax, preventing possible strain and tear. When the muscle relaxes, it gives the foam roller the opportunity to find *hot spots* or trigger points. These areas in the muscle belly may impede nerve conduction and blood flow, which may directly affect performance. Both can be physiological limitations when actively engaged in a sport setting or training environment. The foam roller provides the first step in the tissue-maintenance process, which is to directly address density. This provides a systemic platform for eventually tackling tissue length via passively stretching the muscle. It is important to note that lacrosse balls, softballs, PVC pipe, and other implements may also be used to accomplish this task. Anatomical hot spots should be changed periodically based on the body's ability to accommodate and no longer receive benefit from the applied stressor. Choosing three new areas every other week is a simple way to accomplish this task.

Glute/Hip Rotator

Quad Foam Roll

Latisimus Dorsi Foam Roll

Adductor Foam Roll

Glute Med Release

Softball Knee Gapping

Softball Quad Mobility

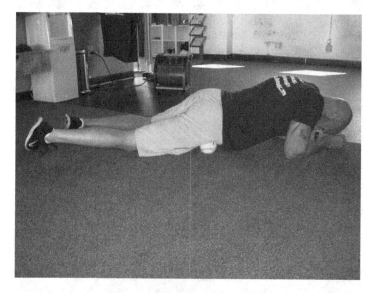

Softball TFL/Rectus Femoris

Med ball Psoas

Peanut Shoulder Flexion

Reset/Activation

Stiffness

A tight muscle may create adjacent imbalance on respective joint structures. In order to restore optimal positioning, the coach programs activation drills that target these anatomical areas and restores appropriate tension within the system. Tension here refers to the tension per unit of change in length. Tension is different than shortness. A short muscle loses its sarcomeres. Visualize two elastic bands; one is short while the other is long. In contrast, a stiff muscle becomes *thicker*. Visualize two elastic bands; they are the same length, but one band is thicker.

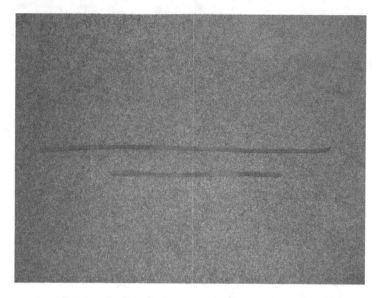

Tissue shortness—in this case, a loss of
sarcomeres makes the muscle short.

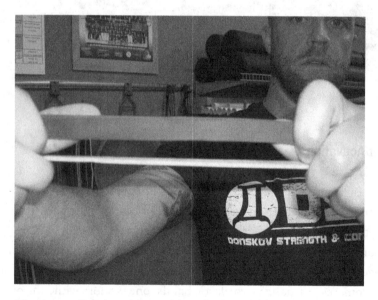

Tension—One band (muscle) is thicker than the other, while
length remains constant. More often than not in the hockey-
playing population tension is the culprit of repetitive movement.

Increased tension is a protective mechanism of the central nervous system (CNS) to avoid injury and protect weak or overused muscle. This mechanism may cause length tension problems, chronic pain, energy leaks, and performance decrements. These weak, overused muscles are referred to as *phasic muscles* and are responsible for big, athletic movements, such as jumping, running, and skating. Tonic muscles, on the other hand, are built for posture. Overtraining and repetitive use typically cause phasic muscles to get weak while simultaneously causing tonic muscles to increase in tension and tightness.

Phasic Versus Tonic Muscles

	Phasic	Tonic
Type	Fast twitch	Slow twitch
Respiration	Anaerobic	Aerobic
Function	Active	Static
Dysfunction	Weaken	Shorten
Treatment	Facilitate	Stretch

Phasic (Prone to Weakness)	Tonic (Prone to Tightness)
Gluteus maximus	Gastroc
Rectus abdominis	Soleus
Serratus anterior	Hamstring
Gluteus medius	Illiopsoas
Anterior tibialis	TFL
Lower trapezius	Rectus femoris
Rhomboids	QL
	Upper trap
	Pec major

Appropriate examples for the competitive hockey player that may show up on an FMS or postural assessment are overactive hip flexors. Hockey is played in a flexed position with the hip flexors constantly engaged under long-duration isometric and concentric load. The hips are responsible for abduction (external rotation, push to the side) during propulsion and adduction (flexing and internally rotating the hip during recovery) as well as the isomeric action of the rectus femoris during single-leg stance on the gliding leg. These continuous demands may cause imbalance in the form of length tension alterations. If a muscle's resting length is compromised, its ability to produce force may be reduced. This affects the efficiency of the stride and may predispose the player to chronic hip issues. In order to offset these demands, an appropriate activation protocol can be set in place.

Adjacent Stiffness

If the hip flexors are constantly facilitated, there is a high probability that the pelvis will be pulled into an anteriorly tipped position. This can cause impingement and mechanical issues within the joint. The practitioner may think of the hip joint as the shoulder joint of the lower body. An anteriorly tipped scapula immediately places the humeral head in a compromised position. Ron Hruska, founder of the Postural Restoration Institute, sums it up eloquently: "Is an acetabulum over a femur any different than an acromion process over a humeral head?" Creating adjacent stiffness of the anterior core musculature can serve to stiffen adjacent structures and reposition the pelvis posteriorly, thereby taking pressure and pull off of the tight, overactive hip musculature. "It is reasonable to think that if these lengthened muscles are activated, thereby resetting the length tension relationship of the muscle spindles, the muscles on the opposite side of the system would begin to let go."[19]

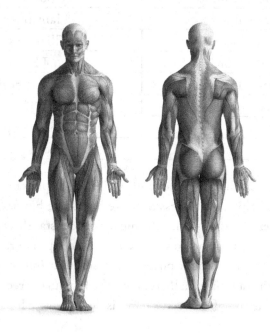

Think of the flexor/adductor complex as a group of muscles that work in direct opposition of the anterior core. This group of muscles attaches at the ASIS, the bottom of the pubis and ischium, and moves the pelvis in an inferior, anterior position. The anterior core has the opposite effect, positioning the pelvis in a superior, posterior direction. Tight, overactive hip flexors/adductors may compromise position, creating a tug-of-war in which the tight, facilitated muscle group always wins. In order to restore tissue length of the flexors/adductors, anterior core stiffness is of utmost importance.

The stiffer/thicker band will always win the tug-of-war battle.

Creating Core Stiffness:

Prone Plank

PRI 90/90 with Balloon: This exercise facilitates the hamstrings and glutes while simultaneously inhibiting the hip flexors. In addition, during each exhalation into the balloon, the ribs internally rotate while the core musculature is facilitated. This is an excellent exercise for hockey players. It takes pressure off the overused anterior hip and repositions the thorax.

Seated Breathing

Lat Hang with Balloon

Long Lever Anti-Rotation targeting the External Oblique

Antagonistic Strength

If muscle tension increases, it is reasonable to think that muscles on the opposite side of the shortened muscle have become lengthened. Reciprocal inhibition states that when a prime mover contracts, the antagonists relax. Continuing on with the example of the hockey player's tight, overactive hip flexors, muscles on the opposite side may become weak and inhibited. A weak and inhibited gluteus maximus can lead to an assortment of lower-extremity issues, such as low back pain, hamstring pulls (although rare in hockey), groin pulls, and femoral anterior glide syndrome. If the glutes cannot perform their duties effectively, the hamstring or adductor magnus may take over as primary extensors, causing potential imbalances and chronic issues for the player. When programming activation/antagonistic strength for hockey players, think of all the muscles that directly oppose the hockey position (muscles that you don't see in the mirror). The gluteus maximus, hamstrings, and posterior shoulder complex provide the hockey player with a balanced approach to resetting appropriate length tension in the system, facilitating these muscles while inhibiting the overworked, overused muscles of the anterior hip and anterior shoulder.

Supported Hip Lift

Unsupported Hip Lift

Tennis Ball Hip Lift

Hip Lift with Leg Extension

Kneeling band Ws for the posterior shoulder. This exercise
promotes shoulder external rotation, retraction, and
posterior tilt of the inferior border of the scapula.

Flexibility/Static Stretching

Tissue Length

Lack of flexibility can directly affect physiology. When a muscle is short, there is a loss of sarcomeres. This loss can affect range of motion around the joint, negatively impact movement quality, alter length-tension relationships, and create inefficient static and dynamic posture. In order to offset these potential problems, incorporating appropriate tissue length protocol is necessary. It is important to note that issues pertaining to tissue length could also be a protective mechanism by the central nervous system to protect weak phasic muscles from injury (see section above). In this case, tension is altered within the system; shortness and tension are two different properties.

When a muscle is elongated, actin fibers move away from myosin filaments placing stretch on the myofiber. This can dampen power output and consequently decrease performance gains.

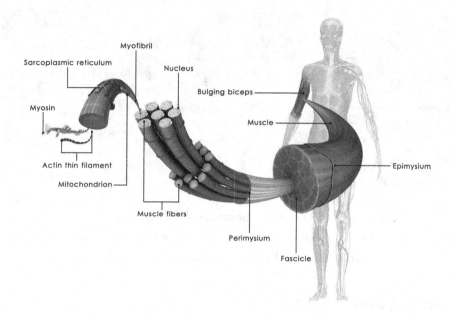

Contraction—Actin and myosin fibers slide over one another, inducing cross-bridge cycling. This shortens the muscle and provides contraction. Stretch—Actin and myosin fibers move away from one another; this lessens the degree of overlap and stretches the tissue.

The important concept for the strength coach to conceptualize is that the placement of the modality, in terms of program design, trumps its potential limitations. It would be unwise to stretch a muscle and immediately perform power work or any other highly demanding central nervous system task. Static stretching may dampen these abilities. If, however, the appropriate progressions listed in table 3.1 are followed, static stretching may serve to increase range of motion around a joint, increase mechanical efficiency, restore appropriate length tension relationships, and provide relief for overworked muscle synergists. Both static and dynamic assessments provide insight into which anatomical areas may be facilitated or inhibited. This information, coupled with the practitioner's understanding of the biomechanics of sport, position, and previous injury history, can provide a solid template for stretching protocol. Based on the demands of the game, the following are several static stretches for hockey players.

Wall Rectus Femoris Stretch

Posterior Hip Stretch

(Psaos Stretch—In order to stretch the psoas, the athlete sets up facing 45 degrees to the box and steps over his or her midline. Stretch is placed on the psoas as the athlete crosses midline based on the insertion of the muscle on the lesser trochanter. Failure to set up properly will fail to stretch this anatomical landmark.)

There has been considerable debate in the strength and conditioning community regarding postexercise foam rolling and static stretching. It is the opinion of the author at this time that both are unnecessary upon the cessation of training. At this point, the muscle has already been damaged at the microscopic level from the eccentric demands of force application. The further increase of stretch causes increased damage and catabolism. A better option for regeneration is a postworkout protein shake, a flush ride to clear any lingering metabolic waste, adequate nutritional intake, and proper sleep. These modalities shift the body into an anabolic state, which is of utmost importance in the recovery process.

Mobility

> Mobility before stability; stability before
> movement ... movement before strength.
> —Gray Cook

Mobility and flexibility are not the same. Mobility is context dependent, meaning that there are different demands placed on the system for different sports and activities, thereby requiring different levels of mobility. Mobility is the ability to reach a desired posture or movement. Flexibility is the range of motion around a joint, many times limited to one to two joints and not heavily reliant on the nervous system for support.

Mobility versus Flexibility

Mobility	Flexibility
□ Joint actions through a wide range of movement	□ Isolated components that affect movement
□ CNS dependent	□ Not system dependent
□ Multiple joints	□ Isolated joints
□ Specific	□ Nonspecific
* Tissue length + neural control + joint architecture = mobility	* Tissue length + joint architecture = flexibility

* Robertson, M. *Flexibility and Mobility for Youth Athletes.* Retrieved from http://www.iyca.org.

There are many factors that affect mobility within the system, such as previous injury, osseous alignment, poor posture, overworked facilitated muscle groups, and poor overall movement quality. These can all affect the system and compromise efficiency. The initial dynamic movement assessment can serve to reveal these inadequacies and prompt the practitioner to program a specific mobility protocol that enhances motor skill (the ability to reach an end goal position efficiently). Mobility protocol follows the joint-by-joint approach set forth by Michael Boyle and Gray Cook.[20]

Joint-by-Joint Approach (Michael Boyle and Gray Cook)

Joint	Required Need
Ankle	Mobility
Knee	Stability
Hip	Mobility
Lumbar spine	Stability
Thoracic spine	Mobility

Scapula	Stability
Glenohumeral joint	Mobility

Increased mobility, enabling the hockey player to express efficient movement within a greater total range, is one of the quickest ways to build faster, more powerful skaters. Elements of relative strength, mobility, and technique are all important aspects in economizing stride mechanics and building more efficient athletes.

Hockey stride = stride length x stride frequency

During the formative years, both stride length and stride frequency may be improved because of the neurological development and the acquisition of improved motor skill and economy. Gaining a useful movement database during the early years of physical literacy advances the learning curve for young athletes. As the hockey player matures in age, the biggest improvement in stride efficiency may be a shift in focus to improving stride length. Stride length is contingent upon several factors, including mobility. Mobility during this time plays a crucial role in realizing these performance gains.

How to Improve Stride Length

Courtesy of Joe DeFranco, EliteFTS Sports Performance Seminar. Technique is dependent on strength and mobility. These elements increase impulse and build stronger skaters. Both elements can be trained in the weight room.

Appropriate mobility of the ankles and hips can directly enhance stride length, which increases efficiency (output relative to the cost of input) and the ability to express force for longer periods of time. This increase in force correlates to faster skaters. Mobility improves impulse. Impulse is the product of force (f) and the time (t) in which it acts. Increasing amplitude and range of motion allows the hockey player to express force for longer periods of time. Mobility has tangible effects on an athlete's ability to enhance acceleration and speed.

$$impulse = force \times \Delta time$$

Equation for Impulse

Acceleration on the ice is a combination of three important variables:
1. Forward lean of the body
2. Positive shin angle, allowing for maximal force production into the ice
3. Fast arms, enabling for quicker turnover of the legs

Ankle Mobility

Ankle Rocks

1   2

Ankle Swings

(1) Ankle swings—This exercise mobilizes the ankle on the frontal plane. The athlete places his or her hands against the wall with the feet facing forward.

(2) Keeping the grounded foot forward, the athlete initiates an ankle swing by swinging the lead back and forth.

Hip Mobility

Hip Rock

Posterior hip rock—The player starts by crossing his or her lead leg in front of the body (if possible parallel to the shoulders). He or she then rocks back into the hip, using a posterolateral sway, creating a posterior hip mobilization. This can be performed for repetitions, time, or breaths.

Diagonal Hip Mobility with Step

Spiderman—This is an excellent hip flexor/adductor mobilization. The player starts in push-up position and steps forward, attempting to step in line with the lead hand. Once this position has been established, the player pushes out on his or her lead leg while dropping the rear leg and engaging the glutes.

1

2

Hip Flexor Mobility

(1) Hip flexor mobility—The athlete sets up with one knee bent on a mat while the other is placed on the wall for leverage.

(2) The athlete leans forward while pulling the rear heel toward the wall. This is an excellent mobility exercise for the rectus femoris, a biarticular muscle used during the hockey stride.

T-Spine Mobility

1   2

T-Spine Rotation

(1) T-spine rotation—The athlete starts with his or her knee bent ninety degrees and resting on the foam roller with the shoulders stacked upon each other.

(2) Slowly moving in a diagonal pattern, the athlete reaches and attempts to touch the floor with the thumb, while maintaining knee position on the roller.

1   2   3

T-Spine Halo

(1) T-spine halo—The athlete starts with the knee bent ninety degrees and resting on the foam roller with the shoulders stacked upon each other. He or she begins by reaching the top hand forward.

(2) The lead hand continues to rotate around the body while maintaining knee position on the foam roller.

(3) End position is reached when the athlete is in full wingspan. The eyes are instructed to follow the lead hand through the full range of motion.

Quadruped T-Spine mobility

Supine Shoulder Flexion with Peanut

Ankle/Hip/Shoulder Mobility

Cook squats (named after physical therapist Gray Cook) are a great exercise for ankle, hip, and shoulder mobility. The athlete starts by touching his or her toes. (Make sure the feet are placed in a "hockey position," as this provides mobility-specific work.) Once the toe touch is complete, the athlete pulls up on his or her toes and sits deeply with the elbows in between the knees. Body weight should be on the midfoot and heel. The athlete reaches toward the ceiling and stands up.

Dynamic Warm-Up

Movement-Based Preparation

The dynamic warm-up is the final piece of the preparation puzzle. After tissue quality, tissue length, mobility, and stability have all been addressed, the athlete is finally ready to partake in a systemic warm-up. The dynamic warm-up enables the athlete to engage in specific motor patterns requiring flexibility, mobility, stability, and coordinated effort. The reader is urged to revisit table 3.1 for appropriate progressions incorporated into designing a user-friendly protocol. The warm-up serves to prepare the central nervous system for the demands of training. Core temperature is increased, as well as heart rate, circulation, and mental acuity. The increase in temperature has a direct effect on muscle pliability, enabling the system to move more efficiently prior to load. The warm-up should also serve to reinforce neuromuscular patterning that the athlete may experience while under stimulus from the barbell or dumbbell prior to use.

If time does not permit, the exercise alone can serve as the dynamic warm-up. For example, *naked bar* complexes prior to Olympic lifting can aid the lifter in preparing for the desired motor pattern and functional range of motion and reinforce muscle coordination patterns. In this instance, the exercise becomes the warm-up.

Linear Warm-up	**Lateral Warm-Up**
Knee hugs	Band break circuit
Quad stretch	Lunge matrix
Leg cradle	Lateral skips
Bear crawls	Cross-over skips
Reverse lunge	Lateral shuffles
SLDL	Carioca
Power skips	Hand crawls
Butt kicks	Low-level bounding
Backpedal	
Happy feet	

Naked Bar Complex (A)	**Naked Bar Complex (B)**
Bottom-Up Approach	*Top-Down Approach*
RDLs	BB snatch
BB row	Front squat
Hang cleans	BB row
Front squat	SLDLs
OH press	

Final Thoughts

Putting It All Together: A Plan of Attack

1. Foam roll—Decrease tissue density and promote circulation. Seek hot spots that may change daily with response to training stress.
2. Reset/activation—Build adequate stiffness and correct any length-tension imbalances.
3. Static stretch—Increase tissue length (if needed).
4. Mobility—Address mobility issues through sound assessment. Increase amplitude and improve impulse.
5. Dynamic warm-up—Initially master the sagittal plane prior to addressing the frontal and transverse planes respectively.

Chapter 4

Bioenergetics: Energy System Demands

> If we know exactly where we're going, exactly how to get there, and
> exactly what we'll see along the way, we won't learn anything.
> —M. S. Peck

Examining the energy system demands in the sport of ice hockey can
lead to equivocal debate. Intragame (player-based decisions) and intergame
(position, game situations) differences all come into context when assessing
which energy system dominates during the course of competitive play.
Context matters. In science, we remove data from context to study and
observe, but it's the context that brings the data to life. Without context, it
is possible to justify or rationalize beliefs and behaviors when in fact most of
the debate simply depends on circumstance. For the team-sport athlete, all
systems of energy production are important in developing and maintaining.

Team Sport: Energy System Requirements

Alactic		Aerobic
←--→		
Football	Hockey	Soccer

*Certainly football and soccer also have aerobic and alactic components,
making these sports alactic/aerobic in nature. Hockey also relies on all systems;
however, the lactic system is also involved during the demands of play.*

Watch the athlete, not the sport. Although shifts can
be as long as 45–60 seconds in length, very rarely does a
player skate at max effort for the entire duration. Small
accelerations are coupled with coasting and gliding, placing
importance on aerobic and alactic qualities.

The average player plays between 12 and 20 shifts per game and has an average rest period of 225 seconds between shifts (Wise, 1993). The rest interval between periods is fifteen minutes. It has been estimated that 70 percent to 80 percent of the energy for a hockey athlete is derived from the alactic and lactic systems (anaerobic).[21]

This does not take away the importance of developing a sound foundation of aerobic fitness, as this can serve to offset exercise-induced metabolic waste and enhance recovery. "All three energy systems are used during an ice hockey game, but one system will predominate, depending on: individual intensity level at that moment (per shift); game situation; and the motivation of the player."[22]

Task-Specific Energy System Demands

Type of Activity	Alactic Anaerobic	Lactic Anaerobic	Aerobic
Five-second burst	85	10	5
Ten seconds of hard skating	60	30	10
Thirty seconds of continuous activity	15	70	15
One-minute shift of intermittent sprints, coasting, and stops	10	60	30
Recovery between shifts/periods	5	5	90

Approximate contribution of the systems during the game of hockey.[23]

Programming Considerations

In Frank Dick's book *Sport Training Principles*,[24] he suggests how different theories of energy system development have influenced numerous coaches over the years. These ideologies have had a strong impact on exercise protocol, exercise prescription, and year-round planning.

Ideology #1

The Sport-Specific Camp

The sport-specific camp argues training should be divided by the percentage breakdown of energy pathways experienced in sport. Shelle et al.[25] and Green et al.[26] quantified the breakdown of energy pathways for ice hockey. They concluded that the anaerobic glycolytic and phosphocreatine (ATP-PC) energy systems provide 69 percent and oxidative phosphorylation 31 percent of the energy demand of ice hockey play.[27] Others have reported similar findings. Thus, based on this ideology, a coach would spend roughly 70 percent of the time developing anaerobic abilities and 30 percent aerobic abilities. This constitutes the sports-specific camp.

Sport	ATP-PC	Glycolysis & Oxidative	Oxidative
Basketball	60	20	20
Fencing	90	10	0
Field Events	90	10	0
Golf Swing	95	5	0
Gymnasitcs	80	15	5
Hockey	50	20	30
Rowing	20	30	50
Running (distance)	10	20	70
Skiing	33	33	33
Soccer	50	20	30
Swimming (distance)	10	20	70
Swimming (50m freestyle)*	40	55	5
Tennis	70	20	10
VolleyBall	80	5	15

Taken from Foss ML and Keteyian S. (1998) The Physiological Basis of Exercise and Sport: 6th Edition

* Stager JM ad Tanner DA. (2005): Swimming, 2nd Edition

Ideology #2

Short, Medium, Long-Term Camp

Another school of thought holds that the sport should be evaluated on its demands relative to short (forty-five seconds to two minutes), medium (two to eight minutes), and long-term endurance (eight or more minutes), as well as speed and strength endurance. Thus, the majority of training should be spent in ideal zones relative to sporting demands. If a hockey player lacks first-step ability, more time would be spent in short-term endurance camp. If the player lacks aerobic power or capacity, more time should be spent in the medium-endurance zone. Most players, using this ideology, would spend very little time in the long-term endurance camp. This constitutes the short, medium, and long-term endurance camps.

Ideology #3
The Aerobic Camp

The final school of thought holds that all endurance-based or team events are founded upon an extensive base of aerobic capacity. Training commences with an accumulation phase in which aerobic development is prescribed. This serves as the prerequisite upon which anaerobic abilities are built and maintained. This constitutes the aerobic camp ideology.

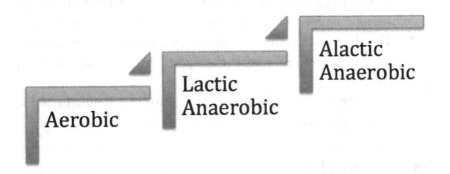

According to Frank Dick, an athlete's training plan may be dictated by the following:

- Competition demands of the sport—referencing the needs analysis is critical in determining the demands of the sport and which qualities the athlete currently lacks. A systemic, periodized plan should be developed in order to create structure and ensure logical motor sequencing; however, the process and daily perturbations in athlete readiness should be used as a means for changing the plan when needed.

- Individual athlete's training status—how long has the player been in a structured strength and conditioning program? Is he or she a beginner, intermediate, or advanced athlete? This can be ascertained during the initial assessment process.
- Stage of development of the athlete (age, gender, anatomy)—which biological windows are open? Are there any training areas to avoid? For example, young athletes ages six to twelve should be encouraged to play multiple sports while focusing on agility, balance, and motor coordination. In addition, intense anaerobic work should be avoided outside the scope of sport. There are significantly lower levels of the glycolytic enzyme phosphofructokinase in the growing child, along with a decreased amount of glycogen stored in the liver and muscle.
- Long- and short-term objectives—what are the long- and short-term objectives or goals for the athlete? How much time does one have to work with him or her? A solid understanding of time commitment is of utmost importance prior to designing the strength and conditioning plan.
- Limitations of the training environment—this includes equipment, appropriate coaching, terrain, weather, and access to facilities.
- The demands of the nonathletic environment—this includes family, relationships, school, other sports, extracurricular activities, and travel.
- The athlete's personality—is the athlete sympathetic or parasympathetic.

Energy Production 101

ATP—The Energy Currency of the Human Body

ATP (adenosine triphosphate) is the energy currency of the human body. It is derived from the conversion of foodstuffs at the muscle cell level and allows the body to convert chemical energy into mechanical output. The breakdown of ATP into ADP + P (adenosine diphosphate + phosphate), or the removal of phosphate, provides the energy required for muscle contraction and performance on the ice. The intramuscular storage of ATP is limited, so in order to maintain contraction, resynthesis is required. If ATP were not to be efficiently replenished, it would quickly be consumed, as only very small amounts are stored within the muscle.

The intramuscular supply of ATP is sufficient to last two seconds, after which resynthesis is necessary. ATP can increase more than a hundredfold in the transition from rest to maximal exercise.[28] The major variable that determines this synthesis of ATP is exercise intensity. Hockey is a metabolically demanding sport, challenging the system to provide appropriate energy during intermittent play, acceleration, deceleration, change of direction, stopping, starting, gliding, and recovery between shifts and periods. It is the ability of the hockey player to regenerate ATP that dictates his or her ability to perform these tasks while maintaining a high-level power output.

ATP regeneration is similar to putting money back into a checking account with a small balance. During the course of a hockey game, the athlete withdraws energy from this account. Failure to reinvest this energy in a timely fashion leads to overdraw penalties or the inability to produce the energy required to compete. In order to keep this account in the green, the ability to produce ATP must be equal to or greater than the energy requirements needed by the player. If the energy requirements are greater than the ability to produce ATP, the account becomes compromised, placing the balance in the red, making further withdrawals difficult.

Balancing the ATP Account

ATP Utilization   ATP Resynthesis

←--→

> *Fatigue occurs when the system becomes imbalanced,* or ATP
> utilization outpaces the ability of ATP resynthesis.

Components of Energy Production

+ *Rate*—The rate is how quickly the energy is being produced. It may also be called the *power of the system.* Each sport requires a certain rate of energy production. Some sports, such as weight lifting and the sprinting disciplines, require immediate energy for very short periods of time, while other sports, such as distance running, require energy for long durations. Team sports like hockey fall somewhere in the middle of this continuum.

+ *Capacity*—This is the duration of time at which the energy is being produced. Different sports require a different time commitment for sustaining power output. Hockey is played for sixty minutes. Depending on player position, time of game, and game situation, forwards may be on the ice for 30 percent of this overall time and defensemen may play upward of 50 percent of this total duration. This places high priority on the ability to sustain high levels of work with minimal fatigue.

Sport Comparison: Energy System Requirements

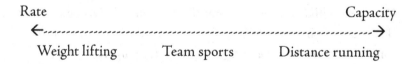

Rate   Capacity

←--→

Weight lifting   Team sports   Distance running

+ *Work-to-rest ratio*—Each sport requires different work-to-rest ratios. In general, sports with a higher anaerobic component require more rest than sports that are aerobic. A higher power output requires additional rest to perform at maximal intensity.

Work-to-Rest Ratio Continuum for Ice Hockey

Neural or Power   Metabolic or Capacity

←---→

Goalie   Forward   Defense

1:4, 1:3, 1:2   1:3, 1:2, 1:1

Depending on game situation, total shots faced, and time played in the defensive zone, goalies need to be both highly alactic and aerobic. They must have the ability to sustain maximal effort for an entire sixty-minute game using the alactic and aerobic systems respectively.

The Aerobic System

The Supply and Recovery System

Think of the aerobic system as your personal checking account.

One can successfully develop a high level of explosive strength in acyclic locomotion only when one possesses sufficiently high aerobic productivity.
—Yuri Verkoshansky

The primary emphasis in the development of endurance should be to decrease the portion of glycolysis in supplying the energy for work and improvement of the muscles' ability to oxidize lactate during work.
—Yuri Verkoshansky

The resynthesis of ATP using aerobic pathways is as follows:

Aerobic ATP production using carbohydrates: 1 unit glycogen + P + ADP + O_2 = 36–38 units ATP + CO_2 + H_2O

Aerobic ATP production using fat: 1 unit free fatty acid + P + ADP + O_2 = 140 units ATP + CO_2 + H_2O

The aerobic system is responsible for sustaining and providing submaximal levels of power output for prolonged periods. It is a supply and recovery system that utilizes oxygen, carbohydrates, and fats to resynthesize ATP and produce mechanical work. Having a strong aerobic foundation can delay the onset of glycolysis from high-intensity anaerobic work and enable the hockey player to recover more efficiently in between shifts and intermissions. Science is reinforcing that aerobic contribution increases as the number of sprints increases within the context of repeated sprint work. A 1993 study by Gaitanos et al. set out to measure the contribution of energy needed to perform ten six-second sprints on a cycle ergometer with thirty seconds' rest between bouts. What the researchers found was that the fall in muscle glycogen was not linear in fashion. "The fall in muscle glycogen concentration during the tenth sprint was less than half that observed during the first sprint and this reduced rate of glycogenolysis occurred despite a high plasma adrenaline concentration." We may conclude that as the number of sprints increases so does the contribution of aerobic metabolism and its ability to regenerate PCr, coupled with a negligible contribution from anaerobic glycolysis.[29] During the demands of a sixty-minute hockey game, the contribution of the aerobic system increases with time. Position-specific demands on the ice utilize the aerobic system at varying capacitates during play.

As hockey is predominantly an anaerobic sport, there is much debate about the need to train the aerobic system. At this time, it is the author's opinion that enhancing the aerobic system's efficiency simultaneously improves many of the limiting factors produced by anaerobic glycolysis (i.e., the oxidation of lactate and pyruvate and the clearance of hydrogen ions), which allow work to continue in the face of changing conditions inside the muscle. In addition, aerobic enhancement gives the player time away from the rigors of year-round high-intensity training. Many times, the goal isn't to simply train the system responsible for play as the anaerobic system adapts and plateaus relatively quickly[30] with a direct increase in maximal glycolytic enzyme kinetics and muscle buffering capacity realized within a two- to three-week time frame. Also working in the glycolytic anaerobic zone is extremely grueling and not sustainable for prolonged blocks of training. A solid foundation of aerobic work not only serves as a favorable prerequisite for building and maximizing efficiency in anaerobic power output but also assists in minimizing fatigue.

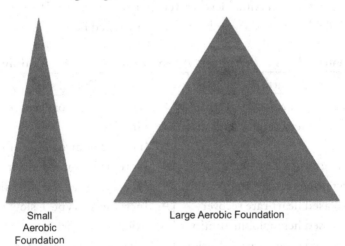

Small
Aerobic
Foundation

Large Aerobic Foundation

Increased Aerobic Efficiency in Ice Hockey

◻ Increase VO2 max (increase in stroke volume via left ventricle eccentric hypertrophy and increased oxygen extraction via an increase in mitochondrial and capillary density).

◻ Increase anaerobic threshold (AnT). This is the point at which the formation of lactate outpaces its clearance, causing muscular fatigue. Anaerobic threshold usually occurs in most people around 60 to 70 percent of VO_2 max. This can be trained, unlike max heart rate.

◻ Increase AnT as a percentage of VO2 max.

- Enhance the ability to oxidize pyruvate, preventing the buildup of lactic acid and hydrogen, essentially limiting muscle contraction.
- Delay declining muscle pH levels.
- Increase recovery.
- Increase parasympathetic tone.

The increased efficiency in the cardiovascular system is a by-product of both central and peripheral adaptations that occur during the course of training. A central adaptation occurs at the heart and lungs and is often referred to as a general adaption. Traditionally, these adaptations take longer to realize (two to three months). In contrast, a peripheral adaptation occurs at the site of the peripheral musculature and is often referred to as a specific adaptation. These adaptations occur much more quickly with the athlete realizing adaptation only after several weeks of training. Peripheral adaptations reach maximal levels after four to six weeks. The central and peripheral adaptations of aerobic training are listed here.

Central Versus Peripheral Adaptations of Aerobic Training

Central	Peripheral
- Eccentric cardiac hypertrophy (left chamber can fill with more blood) - Increased stroke volume - Decreased resting heart rate - Increased heart-rate recovery - Increased hemoglobin affinity - Increased pulmonary diffusion - Parasympathetic drive	- Increase in oxygen enzyme kinetics - Increase in myoglobin affinity - Increase in mitochondria - Increase in capillary density - Increase in type I slow-twitch oxidative efficiency - Increase in type IIa oxidative efficiency

Note—central adaptations are general adaptations; they occur at the heart and lungs. Peripheral adaptations are specific adaptations; they occur at the peripheral musculature.

Methods of Off-Ice Cardiovascular Training

Rhythmic contractions of large muscles at submaximal power outputs (below AnT) are needed to create conditions that favor aerobic pathways.

In this case, both heart rate and VO2 max are increased and an adaptation specific to circulatory function is achieved. It is important for the strength and conditioning professional to realize that many times intense (greater than 85 percent) weight lifting protocols for the hockey player do not fit into this category. In this case, the relationship between heart rate and VO2 max becomes dissociated.

> It is important to recognize that elevated heart rate per se is not the requisite stimulus that drives chronic cardiovascular adaptations. For example, during conventional resistance training, heart rate and VO2 will be dissociated because elevation of the former will occur due to a drive for motor unit recruitment that is mediated by the sympathetic branch of the autonomic nervous system. Furthermore, the intense contractile effort that characterizes each repetition and the corresponding increase in intramuscular pressure will trap blood in peripheral vascular beds, thereby reducing blood flow until the "sticking point" of each repetition is surpassed (Shepherd, 1987). This is not consistent with the specific overload that drives positive cardiovascular adaptation.[31]

Fred Hatfield, in his book *Power: A Scientific Approach*, does a fantastic job reinforcing the physiology:

> Weight training raises heart rate, but restricts venous return of the blood to the heart. This, in turn, causes a decrease stroke volume—less blood is available to be pumped out. The occlusion of venous return is known to cause a "pressor response," which in turn activates certain chemicals (catecholamines) that increase heart rate relative to VO2 uptake. Since stroke volume must be elevated in order for there to be an improvement in cardiorespiratory adaptation, the circulatory restrictiveness of weight training must be reduced if there is to be an improvement in max VO2 uptake to be derived from weight training.[32]

There are several methods used to condition the aerobic system for hockey players. This form of energy system development usually takes place at the onset of the off-season, the general preparation phase, prior to more specific programming. The idea of quantity first, quality later seeks to exploit the aerobic window, build sustainability early in the training program, and give players a break from the demands of the season. It is also a very maintainable modality throughout a player's career. Quality peak training can only be sustained for minimal amounts of time, as it is demanding on the system, both physiologically and emotionally.

Prior to the programming, attaining the athlete's resting heart rate and maximum heart rate can further aid the practitioner in individualizing target heart rate zones. The following are several methods for attaining this information.

- *Resting heart rate* may best be attained in the morning while lying supine. To track your resting heart rate, place a middle/index finger on the radial artery on the wrist and count how many beats occur in a twenty-second window; this number is then multiplied by three to find a resting heart rate.
- *Max heart rate* can be attained in several ways:
- *One-minute go test*—Have the athlete sustain maximal intensity for sixty seconds or to progressive exhaustion. The HR recorded immediately after exercise will be considered maximal heart rate. This is an activity-specific test, which means you may have two different HR readings depending on the tool used for assessment (bike, treadmill, and so on).
- *Interval test*—The athlete performs three thirty-second intervals at maximal intensity, followed by sixty seconds of recovery. Maximal heart rate is determined immediately after the third interval.

Heart rate zones are programmed using the Karvonen Index.

Karvonen Index: (MHR - RHR) x (Int. %) + RHR

Assume a coach wants to prescribe aerobic training at 60 percent of the athlete's VO2 max. If the athlete has a resting heart rate of 55 beats per minute (bpm) and a max heart rate of 200 bpm, he or she will train with an intensity of 142 bpm.

$$55 + (200 - 55) \times .60 = 142 \text{ bpm}$$

+ *Cardiac Output*—Rhythmic submaximal contractions of the large muscle groups for a long duration fit the criteria for cardiac output work. Depending on the time of year, various modalities (running, biking, swimming, aerobic circuit) and tools can be used to accomplish aerobic conditioning. This form of training usually occurs during the transition phase immediately following the hockey season or early in the preparation phase as general preparation work commences.

Method	Target	Guidelines	Rest	Volume	Frequency
Cardiac output	Eccentric cardiac hypertrophy	HR 65–75% VO2	N/A	30–90 min.	1–3 sessions/week

Table Adapted from J. Jamieson, Ultimate MMA Conditioning *Ref. Chap. 4, 38/39

+ *Tempo Runs*—Tempo runs are a great method to open up the hips and build a solid base of general endurance during the early stages of the off-season. Running is excellent for hockey players, as it serves to open up the hips and counter the repetitive flexion experienced while maintaining optimal hockey position. An athlete could run the length of a football field (110 yards), walk the width of the end zone for recovery, and repeat his or her effort. Extra density may be attained by adding calisthenics (push-ups, core work) between tempo runs as a way for the coach to increase volume without pounding the joints. The coach instructs the athletes to run at intensity between a light jog and all-out sprint. Volume is slowly increased each week 10 to 20 percent.

Method	Target	Guidelines	Rest	Volume	Frequency
Tempo runs	Eccentric hypertrophy, increase slow-twitch fiber capacity	HR 65–75% VO2	Width of end zone	X8–16+	1–3 sessions/week

+ **Sled Marches/Drags**—Sled marches are an efficient exercise to build aerobic efficiency and to strengthen drive force into the ground. This is a concentric-only exercise and can be used at various times in the training process without delayed soreness. Early in the training process, the sled may be used to focus on mechanics, aerobic capacity, and recovery, while later in the process, the sled may be used to build alactic qualities by deloading the sled and sprinting. An area of fifteen to twenty yards is used as the player simply pushes or drags the sled in a marching pattern, focusing on punching the lead knee forward and then driving the leg down underneath the hip, producing both horizontal and vertical forces and propelling the sled forward. The athlete can focus on both aerobic conditioning and sprint mechanics simultaneously. The sled enables the player to increase impulse and improve force production. The sled is a great alternative to hill sprinting, having similar ground-contact patterns. Loading should be heavy enough to permit forward lean and light enough to allow complete extension of the hips.

Method	Target	Guidelines	Rest	Volume	Frequency
Sled march/drag	Increase slow-twitch hypertrophy, improve sprint mechanics	HR 65–75% VO2	1–3 minutes	X4–12 + (15 yards)	1–2 sessions/week

+ **Aerobic circuit**—Aerobic circuits are designed to build adequate levels of general muscle endurance. Based on the method of PHA (peripheral heart action), rotation of body parts during the circuit is of importance (e.g., upper body, lower body, core, and so on).

This idea stems from the understanding that when a muscle is stimulated, its capillary beds dilate, which increases blood flow to the targeted area. The idea behind PHA is that it may essentially send blood from one are of the body to another. If sequenced properly, this may reduce fatigue and help the athlete maintain quality work throughout the duration of the circuit.

Method	Target	Guidelines	Rest	Volume	Frequency
Aerobic circuit	Improve oxidative capacity of slow-twitch muscles, build general endurance	Pick 5–6 exercises performed for time (30–45 seconds on and 15 seconds off), keep HR in aerobic zone	N/A	X25–30 Frequency depends on number of exercises/ circuits	1–2 sessions/week

+ *Aerobic Power Intervals*—MacDougall and Sale advocate high-intensity aerobic interval training to increase the oxidative capacity of both type I and type II fibers.[33] This allows for the efficient removal of metabolic by-products and serves to delay anaerobiosis. This method of aerobic development seeks to increase cardiac strength. Stronger contractions from the heart aid in getting oxygen-rich blood to the working muscle, delaying fatigue and increasing performance on the ice.

Method	Target	Guidelines	Rest	Volume	Frequency
Aerobic power intervals	Cardiac strength, oxidative capacity of both type I, and IIa fibers	1–2 minutes high intensity (below AnT)	2–5 minutes (HR 120–130)	X4–12	1–2 sessions/week

Table Adapted from J. Jamieson, Ultimate MMA Conditioning *Ref. Chap. 4, 38/39

+ *Threshold Training*—Maximal heart rate is largely genetically predetermined, does not improve with training, is sport-specific in nature, and declines with age in sedentary populations. Threshold training seeks to increase the anaerobic threshold as a percentage of maximal heart rate while delaying the onset of lactate formation. Threshold training seeks to increase the oxidative efficiency of both muscle-fiber types and power output at lactate threshold.

Method	Target	Guidelines	Rest	Volume	Frequency
Threshold training	Oxidative efficiency, power at AnT	5–10 minutes at HR +-5/AnT	1–5 minutes	X3–5	1–2 sessions/week

Table Adapted from J. Jamieson, Ultimate MMA Conditioning *Ref. Chap. 4, 38/39

Review

The aerobic system is a supply and recovery pathway necessary for the production of energy and the removal of chemical by-products associated with high-intensity work. Hockey is an intermittent game of acceleration, deceleration, change of direction, and high-impact collisions. Although the alactic and lactic systems are predominately involved, having a strong aerobic foundation supports these metabolic pathways and allows them to work more efficiently. Lactate formation is unavoidable and fluctuates during the course of a sixty-minute hockey game. Shift length, position, ice time, and rest are all elements that affect the formation of lactate. Noonan et al. tested six Division I ice hockey players during selected shifts in the first and third periods of a sixty-minute hockey game. The researchers found blood lactate levels fluctuated, ranging from 4.4 to 13.7 mmol.L with a mean value of 8.15 (+2.72) mmol.L.[34] Having a strong aerobic fitness level can change the fate of lactate. Lactic acid is removed from the body in several different ways, all of which are contingent on the efficiency of the aerobic system.

+ Muscle lactate is disposed of first by oxidation to pyruvate and then by the dissimilation to carbon dioxide and water.[35]
+ Some of the blood lactate is taken up by the liver, which reconstructs it to glycogen via the Cori cycle.[36]

- The remaining blood lactate diffuses back into the muscle or other organs to be oxidized and dissimilated. This oxidation of lactate causes the formation of carbon dioxide, which is mostly reconstructed blood bicarbonate, before being excreted by the lungs.[37]

Aerobic work is general in nature and should be placed in either the transition block immediately after the demands of a long hockey season, the general preparation block at the onset of the off-season, or used in miniblocks throughout the course of the year to stimulate recovery and regeneration. In addition, the use of aerobic conditioning is less taxing on the body and gives the hockey player time away from the demands of high-intensity work, which is grueling both physically and mentally and unsustainable throughout the entire course of the calendar year. As strength and rehabilitation expert Darcy Norman states, "A good rule of thumb is that an athlete in a long, slow sport such as long-distance running needs more speed work to be successful. An athlete in a start-and-stop sport probably needs more long, slow work without the extra impact, such as cycling, to build the engine to be better able to sustain the intensity and repetitiveness of the sport." For a more in-depth analysis of energy system methodology, the reader is urged to read Joel Jamieson's book entitled *Ultimate MMA Conditioning*.[38]

The Anaerobic Lactate System

Think of your lactate system as cash in your pocket. It's quicker to access than a personal checking account (aerobic system) but limited in capacity for long-term use.

> Most part of sport games has alactic-aerobic character of the energy supplying during the matches. In team sports where the competition rules provide for the substitution of players during the game (especially in hockey), the glycolytic energy supply has fundamental importance.
> —Yuri Verkoshansky

The resynthesis of ATP using glycolytic pathways is as follows:

Lactate: Glycogen + P + ADP -→ ATP (3 units) + lactate

Lactate: Glucose + P + ADP -→ ATP (2 units) + lactate

The lactic system supports maximum power output for approximately 15 to 120 seconds. This system is of extreme importance in the sport of ice hockey. The lactate system is anaerobic in nature (does not use oxygen) and breaks down carbohydrates to resynthesize ATP at a much faster rate than by aerobic production. It does so by the dissimilation of glycogen to glucose, glucose to pyruvate, and finally pyruvate to lactate. Pyruvate accumulates because the capacity of the mitochondria to oxidize it is outpaced by its production. This, in turn, causes lactate formation. As strength and conditioning expert Joel Jamieson states, "The key role of lactate means it essentially acts like an energy bridge between anaerobic and aerobic metabolism."[39] The efficiency of the aerobic system cannot be ignored, as sufficient oxygen can change lactate back into pyruvate and delay the onset of fatigue.

The disadvantage of this system is that it cannot sustain power output for prolonged periods of time, as the formation of hydrogen and lactate reduce pace and inhibit muscle contraction capabilities. Lactate inhibits calcium release, which is critical in muscle contraction. In addition, as mentioned previously, this form of training is extremely grueling on the body and cannot be sustained for long durations in the off-season. Frank Dick defines strength endurance, as "training to develop the athletes' ability to apply force in the climate of lactic anaerobiosis." He further warns,

"Strength endurance training causes considerable wear and tear in the athletes' organism, and it is possible that a saturation of microcycles with units of this type would cause a loss of mental and physical resilience"[40] Like any other method, anaerobic lactate training is a powerful tool, but its use must be carefully placed into a structured strength and conditioning program. It is not recommended to use this form of conditioning for longer than four to six weeks in time, preferably the month before the season begins, with a frequency of no more than four times per week. The central and peripheral adaptations of anaerobic training are listed here.

Central Versus Peripheral Adaptations of Anaerobic Training

Central	Peripheral
<ul><li>Left ventricle concentric hypertrophy</li><li>Rate coding</li><li>Motor unit recruitment</li><li>Intermuscular coordination</li><li>Intramuscular coordination</li><li>Sympathetic drive</li></ul>	<ul><li>Increase glycolytic enzyme kinetics (glycogen phosphorylase, hexokinase, glycogen phosphofructinase)</li><li>Decrease capillary density</li><li>Increase in type 2a oxidative efficiency</li></ul>

Central adaptations are general adaptations and occur at the heart and lungs. Peripheral adaptations are specific adaptations and occur in the peripheral musculature.

Methods of Off-Ice Anaerobic Lactate Training

Shifting the focus from aerobic training to anaerobic training means manipulating the work-to-rest ratio. As a general rule, the more intense the workload, the shorter it can be sustained and the longer the rest needed for adequate recovery. The opposite holds true for less-intense workloads where sustainability is longer in duration and the rest periods between bouts are shorter.

Lactate Power
Slide Board Intervals

Lactate power intervals are designed to increase lactate ATP production during anaerobiosis by the breakdown of muscle glycogen. The slide board is an effective tool in the hockey player's toolbox. The slide board is efficient in targeting the major muscles of the hip and lower back (hip flexors, hip extensors, adductors, abductors, and lumbar spine). The recovery leg during the hockey stride is in an open chain position (off the ground), and many times, players have a tendency to under strengthen and overstretch the muscles responsible for this duty. The sideboard taxes the hip flexors/adductors in a closed-chain motion as both eccentric and concentric forces are being applied. It would be difficult for the practitioner to find another piece of equipment that can do the same during one single repetition! Slide board training is an excellent form of conditioning for hockey players in the off-season. During the regular season, slide boards can be used to train the upper extremity. For fear of overuse injuries of the hip musculature during the hockey season, slide board use is not recommended.

Method	Target	Guidelines	Rest	Volume	Frequency
Lactate power: slide board intervals	Increase ATP production using the lactate system	20–40 seconds (max effort)	1–3 minutes	X6–12 reps	1–2 sessions/week

Tables Adapted from J. Jamieson, Ultimate MMA Conditioning *Ref. Chap. 4, 38/39

Lactate Capacity Intervals

This form of training is demanding in nature and seeks to increase the ability of the hockey player to sustain maximal power output while buffering metabolic by-products, such as hydrogen and lactate. Hockey players can use multiple forms of equipment with this method of training. Slide board intervals and running intervals, such as the four-hundred-meter run and the three-hundred-yard shuttle can all be used to attain this physiological response.

Method	Target	Guidelines	Rest	Volume	Frequency
Lactate capacity	Increase buffering capacity (the ability to maintain output in anaerobic conditions	60–120 seconds	45 seconds to 2 minutes of incomplete rest	X3 reps 2–3 series	1–2 sessions/week

In order to maintain quality power output and replenish fuel, it may be advisable to split the total repetitions into a few series consisting of two to three reps each. The longest rest interval (five to ten minutes) is planned between the sets so that the accumulated lactic acid will have sufficient time to oxidize and the athlete may start the new workload fresh and nearly recovered.[41]

Review

The anaerobic lactate system is responsible for producing ATP without the aid of oxygen. It accomplishes this task with the breakdown of glycogen and glucose. This metabolic pathway can produce power at a much more efficient rate but cannot sustain this power for long durations without excessive fatigue and muscle soreness. This form of training is appropriate in the final stages of the preparation block prior to the season commencing. If the coach has limited time with the athlete during the off-season, this method of training may occur during earlier stages. As hockey strength and conditioning expert Jack Blatherwick explains, "This training is difficult and stressful and should be limited to a few weeks before the season."[42] Vladimir Issurin echoes these comments and states, "Workloads that elicit lactate accumulation over 8mM are intended to enhance anaerobic glycolytic power and capacity; they contribute greatly to the program in the final stages prior to the target competition."[43] The lactate system adapts and plateaus relatively quickly and does not need to be trained year-round or for large blocks of training (longer than six weeks). As strength and condition expert Derek Hansen states, "Every training element has a point of diminishing returns. Our job (the coach's job) is to find it, shift emphasis and cycle back at the optimal point in time." This system is specific to the demands of the game and is very important for the hockey player to be exposed to during a well-planned strength and conditioning program.

The Anaerobic Alactic System

Think of the alactic system as a credit card. It's quicker to use than cash, and less time-consuming than accessing one's checking account. However, in order to use it, one must have sufficient funds in one's account.

The resynthesis of ATP using the alactic or ATP-PC pathway is as follows:

$$ADP + P + P \text{ (from the breakdown of PC)} \rightarrow ATP$$

The anaerobic alactic pathway, otherwise known as the ATP-PC pathway, is the quickest manner in which the body resynthesizes ATP for immediate energy. This is due in large part to three different variables:

1) Phosphocreatine (PCr) is immediately available in the muscle.
2) No oxygen is needed.
3) Very few chemical reactions take place. Phosphocreatine is split into creatine and phosphate with help from the enzyme creatine

kinase. ADP and P join with the remaining phosphate to produce ATP for immediate use.

The alactic system is responsible for immediate, explosive bursts of energy, lasting approximately six to fifteen seconds. This intense work is not sustainable for prolonged periods of time, as the rate of ATP utilization outpaces the rate of ATP resynthesis. PCr store in muscle can provide up to three times the amount of the stored ATP and can do so in around ten seconds. The PCr store is returned to near resting levels in about sixty to ninety seconds, making PCr a reusable fuel.[44] Full replenishment may take three to five minutes. This system works hand in hand with the aerobic system. A strong foundational aerobic base serves to recover and regenerate PCr stores efficiently, enabling a player to repeat power output while maintaining performance. Both the aerobic and alactic systems continue to contribute ATP during repeated sprints in the face of acidosis.[45] The relationship between the alactic and aerobic system can be taken one step further, as both methods are trained without the buildup of acidosis.

Methods of Off-Ice Anaerobic Alactic Training

It is important to remember to keep the duration of work short (about six to fifteen seconds) when training this system. Although all three energy systems are being used, longer work bouts can lead to the reliance on glycolysis and thus increase acidosis in the working muscle. This should be minimized when training in the alactic zone. In addition, sufficient rest is needed to replenish PCr stores and maintain quality performance. When training the alactic pathway, think quality first, quantity second. A minimum of about sixty to ninety seconds is needed to replenish PCr stores and maintain quality power output.

Alactic Power Intervals

Alactic power intervals can be accomplished in multiple ways, including ten- to fifty-meter runs, hill sprints, explosive medicine-ball work, sled sprints (linear and lateral), and plyometrics are just a few methods that seek to attack the alactic window of energy production. The introduction to series strategically placed in between working sets allows for optimal fuel replacement and the maintenance of quality work.

Method	Target	Guidelines	Rest	Volume	Frequency
Alactic power intervals	Increase alactic enzymes (creatine kinase)	6–10 seconds	1–3 minutes	X5–6 reps, 1–2 series/ workout	1–3 sessions/week

Table Adapted from J. Jamieson, Ultimate MMA Conditioning *Ref. Chap. 4, 38/39

In order to maintain quality power output and replenish fuel, it may be advisable to split the total repetitions into a few series consisting of five to six reps each. The longest rest interval (five to ten minutes) is planned between the sets so that the accumulated metabolic byproducts have sufficient time to be oxidized, the athlete may remain fresh, and to ensure quality power output may be maintained.[46]

Alactic Capacity Intervals

Alactic capacity is extremely important for team sports. Methods of training are similar in nature to alactic power work, although work bouts are slightly longer in duration and rest intervals are incomplete, challenging the aerobic system's efficiency. Fifty to one-hundred-meter runs, hill sprints, explosive medicine-ball work, sled sprints (linear and lateral), and plyometrics are just a few methods that seek to attack the alactic window of energy production. The introduction to series strategically placed in between working sets allows for optimal fuel replacement and the maintenance of quality work.

Method	Target	Guidelines	Rest	Volume	Frequency
Alactic capacity intervals	Increase PCr storage capacity	Ten to fifteen seconds	Incomplete rest ~ 20–90 seconds	X10–12 reps, 1–2 series/ workout	1–3 sessions/week

Table Adapted from J. Jamieson, Ultimate MMA Conditioning *Ref. Chap. 4, 38/39

In order to maintain quality power output and replenish fuel, it may be advisable to split the total repetitions into a few series consisting of five to six reps each. The longest rest interval (five to ten minutes) is planned between the sets so that the accumulated metabolic by-products have sufficient time to be oxidized, the athlete may remain fresh, and to ensure quality power output may be maintained.[47]

Review

Chasing the energy system is the same as chasing pain. Many times the problem is the efficiency of the supporting structures and pathways.
—Anthony Donskov

The anaerobic alactic system is responsible for producing ATP without the use of oxygen. It accomplishes this task with the breakdown of intramuscular creatine phosphate and the assistance of the enzyme creatine kinase. This metabolic pathway is the fastest way to resynthesize ATP; however, it cannot sustain output for long periods of time, as ATP utilization exceeds ATP resynthesis. This form of training is appropriate during the early to middle portions of the preparation block. It can be simultaneously programmed with aerobic training, as both pathways are dependent upon one another and do not place the muscle in a state of acidosis. Acidosis inhibits muscle contraction via interference with the enzyme creatine kinase. As hockey strength and conditioning expert Jack Blatherwick states, "We should train like racehorses, not plow horses."[48] The alactic system is necessary for the short bursts of speed and acceleration that define the game of hockey. This system is crucial for the hockey player to expose through purposeful training.

Putting It All Together: Building an Energy System Plan

General <----------------> Specific
Central <----------------> Peripheral

The end goal of a structured strength and conditioning program is to build a plan that slowly moves toward the required demands of the sport. Many factors play a part in the programming process, variables such as competition schedule, time allotment with the athlete, training age, training goals, and overall stage of athletic development. The training calendar can be broken into three categories: transition, preparation, and competition (more in chapter 6).

Transition (regeneration) is the time frame immediately following the hockey season, which leads into the preparation phase of the off-season. For the hockey player, this is typically the month of April.

Preparation (adaptation)—The preparation period, also known as the off-season, is when the majority of off-ice strength and conditioning gains take place. The preparation block can be further divided into the general preparation (May to June) and the specific physical preparation period (July to August). This is known as the preseason.

Competition (application)—The competition block, known as the in-season is September to March. The game schedule is dependent on the league and caliber of the player. Elite National Hockey League players play eighty-two games per season. This high volume of hockey makes this period a difficult time to overtax the athlete in the weight room. In comparison, a Division I college hockey player may play thirty-four games per season, allowing the coach to be more aggressive during in-season periods.

Each block (transition, preparation, and competition) is determined by the overall length of the competitive hockey season. Players with long playoff runs may have less overall time to spend preparing during the off-season when compared to players and teams that don't make the playoffs. The following is a continuum of energy system demands for hockey players. Early in the training process, aerobic qualities are taxed. This gives the player quality rest after the demands of a long season while focusing on improving the efficiency of the circulatory system, in particular, the central adaptations of the heart. During the mid- and latter portions of the preparation period, alactic training may commence. Both aerobic and alactic conditioning work as favorable partners, the former as a supply and recovery system, the latter as a system that provides immediate ATP for explosive effort. Both systems are taxed without the buildup of acidosis. This process may be known as what strength coach Mike Robertson refers to as "working the V." Working the V means working opposite ends of the continuum and slowly progressing toward middle ground; the longer the off-season, the more obtuse the angle and the wider the V. Short off-season periods produce the opposite effect—acute angles and a much narrower V. The V slowly narrows and training shifts to more lactate work as training camp approaches. During this time special physical preparation should take place and embraced a shift toward energy demands that have a strong correlation to sporting demands. The peripheral adaptations of the lactate system are trained approximately three to six weeks prior to the commencement of training camp. The time course for these enzymatic adaptations in glycolytic kinetics, such as an increase in phosphorylase, hexokinase, and phosphofructinase do not take nearly as long as adaptations that affect structural proteins, such as increase in myofibrils, mitochondrial density, and cardiac volume. In addition, this form of training is demanding both physiologically and psychologically and should be avoided for prolonged blocks of training without adequate recovery and regeneration.

Work the V

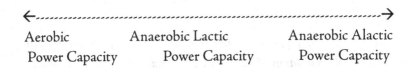

Aerobic	Anaerobic Lactic	Anaerobic Alactic
Power Capacity	Power Capacity	Power Capacity

Hockey is sport where all energy systems are used throughout the course of a sixty-minute game. When viewing the training process as a continuum from general to specific both aerobic and alactic systems are trained first, while the anaerobic lactate system is trained during later blocks of the periodized plan. This may also be known as "working the V." These blocks act as favorable prerequisites, focus on both power and capacity of the respective system, and move from central (general) to peripheral (specific) in nature.

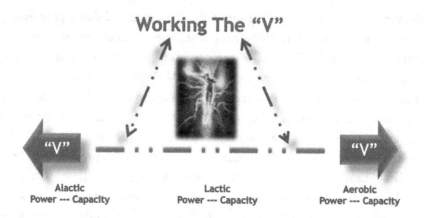

Working The "V"

"V" ← Alactic
Power --- Capacity

Lactic
Power --- Capacity

"V" → Aerobic
Power --- Capacity

Working the V during a long off-season. The shorter the time frame, the more acute the angle and the quicker the exposure to the energy demand of the sport.

Aerobic	Anaerobic
Volume first	Intensity first
Intensity second	Volume second

Early in the training plan, volume precedes intensity with an emphasis on central adaptation. As the season approaches, the hockey player focuses on energy system work more closely resembling game energetics. In this case, intensity is increased, followed by the ability to display the same intensity for longer durations of time, using anaerobic means.

Potential Off-Season Energy System Periodization Scheme for Hockey Players

Block	Goals	Calander	Methods
Transision/Preparation	General Cardiac endurance Improve aerobic capacity. Vascular development. Stroke volume and oxidative capacity of slow twitch fibers.	Early May-April 4-6 week block	Cardiac Output Tempo Runs Sled March/Drags Aerobic Circuit
General Preparation	General power/cardiac endurance Increase aerobic power and contratile properties of the heart while increasing anaerobic threshold. Increase PCr stores and the efficiency of alactic enzymes.	May-June 4-6 week block	Cardiac Power Intervals Threshold Training Alactic Power Alactic Capactiy
Special Preparation/Hockey Specific	Increase game specific power output while mimimizing fatigue. Increaese efficiency while buffering lactate. Game day conditioning.	July-August 4 week block	Lactate Power Lactate Capacity

	Modality	Reps	Run	Rest
Phase 1				
Week 1				
Day 1	Tempo Run 110's	x10	:15	:45-:60
Day 2	Cardicac Output 45 min. Bike, rollerblade, Eliptical	HR (120-150bpm)		
Day 3	Tempo Run 110's	x10	:15	:45
Day 4	2 mile Run		20 min.	
Week 2				
Day 1	Tempo Run 110's	x12	:15	:45-:60
Day 2	Cardicac Output 50 min. Bike, rollerblade, Eliptical	HR (120-150bpm)		
Day 3	Tempo Run 110's	x12	:15	:45
Day 4	2 mile Run		18 min.	
Week 3				
Day 1	Tempo Run 110's	x14	:15	:45-:60
Day 2	Aerobic Circuit 30 min.	x30		
		HR (120-150)		
Day 3	Tempo Run 110's	x14	:15	:45
Day 4	2.5 mile Run		22 min.	
Week 4				
Day 1	Tempo Run 110's	x16	:15	:45-:60
Day 2	Aerobic Circuit 35 min.	x35		
		HR (120-150)		
Day 3	Tempo Run 110's	x16	:15	:45
Day 4	2.5 mile Run		20 min.	

	Modality	Reps	Run	Rest
Phase 2				
Week 5				
Day 1	Cardiac Power Intervals	x4	1:00	4:00
Day 2	Hill Sprints OR Incline Treadmill	x20	:05	:55
Day 3	Tempo Runs	x18	:15	:45
Day 4	Hill Sprints OR Incline Treadmill	x20	:05	:55
Week 6				
Day 1	Cardiac Power Intervals	x6	1:00	3:00
Day 2	Hill Sprints OR Incline Treadmill	x22	:05	:55
Day 3	Tempo Runs	x18	:15	:45
Day 4	Hill Sprints OR Incline Treadmill	x22	:05	:55
Week 7				
Day 1	Cardiac Power Intervals	x8	1:00	3:00
Day 2	Hill Sprints OR Incline Treadmill	x25	:05	:55
Day 3	OFF Day			
Day 4	Hill Sprints OR Incline Treadmill	x25	:05	:55
Week 8				
Day 1	Cardiac Power Intervals	x10	1:00	2:00
Day 2	Hill Sprints OR Incline Treadmill	x28	:05	:55
Day 3	OFF Day			
Day 4	Hill Sprints OR Incline Treadmill	x28	:05	:55

	Modality	Reps	Run	Rest
Phase 3				
Week 9				
Day 1	Cardiac Power Intervals	x12	1:00	2:00
Day 2	Sled Sprints	x10	:10	:45
Day 3	Cardiac Power Intervals	x12	1:00	2:00
Day 4	Sled Sprints	x10	:10	:45
Week 10				
Day 1	Cardiac Power Intervals	x12	1:00	2:00
Day 2	Sled Sprints	x12	:10	:45
Day 3	Tempo Runs	x18	:15	:45
Day 4	Sled Sprints	x12	:10	:45
Week 11				
Day 1	Tempo Runs	x18	:15	:45
Day 2	Sled Sprints	x14	:10	:45
Day 3	Tempo Runs	x18	:15	:45
Day 4	Sled Sprints	x14	:10	:45
Week 12				
Day 1	Tempo Runs	x18	:15	:45
Day 2	Sled Sprints	x16	:10	:45
Day 3	Tempo Runs	x18	:15	:45
Day 4	Sled Sprints	x16	:10	:45

	Modality	Reps	Run	Rest
Phase 4				
Week 13				
Day 1	Slide Board	x6	:30	1:00
Day 2	Explosive Repeats	x6	:20	:30
Day 3	Slide Board	x6	:30	1:00
Day 4	Explosive Repeats	x6	:20	:30
Week 14				
Day 1	Slide Board	x8	:30	1:00
Day 2	Explosive Repeats	x8	:20	:30
Day 3	Slide Board	x8	:30	1:00
Day 4	Shuttle Rums	x4	:30	1:30
	125 yard Shuttle (25 yrds apart)			
Week 15				
Day 1	Slide Board	x10	:30	1:00
Day 2	Explosive Repeats	x10	:20	:30
Day 3	Slide Board	x10	:30	1:00
Day 4	Shuttle Rums	x6	:30	1:30
	125 yard Shuttle (25 yrds apart)			
Week 16				
Day 1	Slide Board	x10	:30	1:00
Day 2	Tempo Runs	x18	:15	:45
Day 3	Slide Board	x10	:30	1:00
Day 4	Tempo Runs	x18	:15	:45
Week 17	Deload and prepare for training camp			

Note—Anaerobic (alactic and lactic) power is sequenced prior to anaerobic capacity. Athletes need to learn to be fast first and then sustain that pace as distance and time increases. Sprint Coach Charlie Francis states, "I believed that stamina was important, but only at a given velocity ... It is easier for sprinters to add distance at a set speed than to step up their speed at a set distance of 200 or 300 meters." Although hockey players are not sprinters, the same logic applies.

Energy system development in hockey is a balance between competing demands, as all systems are used at varying degrees during certain portions of the game. These systems should also be stimulated during the off-season to properly prepare the player for the demands of the sport. "High-Intensity training produces a potent stimulus for muscle cell hypertrophy, that appears to be mediated via increased protein synthesis. Conversely, an oxidative endurance training stress causes muscle to respond in an opposite fashion by ultimately degrading myofibril protein to optimize the kinetics of oxygen uptake."[49] The key is to choose the appropriate modality during each block of training to allow the systems to work efficiently, slowly moving from general to specific with minimal overlap and interference. Miniblocks may be added during prolonged work periods to reintroduce a system that needs additional work or has not been trained for a considerable period of time.

Chapter 5

Power Training for Hockey

Power is the ability to perform work as quickly as possible. Power is rate-dependent (how quickly the light switch turns on) motor ability, as opposed to force, which is more dependent on magnitude (how brightly the light can shine). It can be defined in several different ways:

P = w/t (work/time)
P =f x d/t (force x distance/time)
P = f x v (force x velocity)
P= s/t (strength/time)

As Fred Hatfield explains, "If we keep distance constant, we can substitute strength for force since the force comes from your strength. Therefore the formula can be written: P = S/T, i.e., the greater the amount of strength that you can display in a certain period of time, the greater will be your explosiveness."[50]

The Force-Velocity Curve

The force-velocity relationship was conceptualized from the ideas of A.V. Hill in 1953.[51] Hill isolated the calf muscles from frog cadavers and stimulated them to perform isotonic contractions (same tension throughout as muscle length changes). What he found was that when he increased the wattage (magnitude of the light), the rate of muscle shortening or velocity (how quickly the light switch turns on) decreased. Thus, the force-velocity relationship was born.

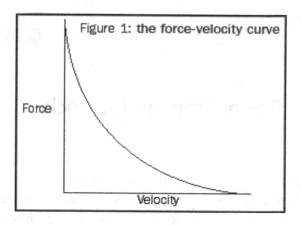

Figure 1: the force-velocity curve

Force

Velocity

Concentric Contraction—As velocity increases, force decreases. This is due to the cycling rate of myosin. Myosin must detach and reattach to actin during high-velocity movement. This decreases force.

Eccentric contraction—As velocity increases, force increases. This is due to the stretch of the elastic components (epimysium, perimysium, endomysium, sarcolemma, and tendon).

Strength and conditioning expert Coach Cal Dietz suggests that this hyperbolic curve may not tell us the full story regarding its application during certain dynamic movements.

> When looking at explosive dynamic movement, its application falls short. You see the curve failed to include one huge variable that is pertinent to sport performance— the series elastic component of dynamic contraction. When you include the extra energy supplied by the stretch shortening cycle during full speed dynamic movements, points one and two from above 1.) Velocity of movement is inversely proportionate to load, 2.) It is impossible to exert high force with fast movements, are incorrect.[52]

When further interpreting the curve for strength coaches and for overlaying the motor qualities that one may program, traditional power work, with the exception of true plyometrics, falls toward the right of the curve. We can interpret the far right of the curve as the sport itself, in this case, hockey.

Intensity Level: force = mass x acceleration

Force   Velocity

←--→

Suitable Training Methods

> Max Strength
> Hypertrophy
> General Strength
> Plyometrics
> Strength Speed
> Speed Strength
> Sport

Mass Dependent   **Acceleration Dependent**

The force velocity continuum and its relationship with suitable strength training methods, modified from King, 1998–2011.[53]

Thoughts on the Force-Velocity Curve for Hockey Players

1) All components along the curve are important to have in a structured strength and conditioning program.

2) Strength is a prerequisite for power (P=f x d/t). By increasing max strength, we can provide a solid foundation for power production. Max strength is the foundational motor ability upon which additional abilities are built. You can't shoot a cannon out of a canoe.

3) Most hockey players spend too much time on the right of the curve (play too many hockey games). Shifting focus to the left side can aid in substantial gains and an increase in durability.

4) Noticeable gains are made in youth populations by shifting the focus to force development.

5) Methods of training used are based on the competition schedule, time of year, and training age of the athlete.

6) Most college hockey players have been exposed to structured strength and conditioning programs (i.e., have spent time along various points in the curve). However, major junior players may lack the physical

development, as the game schedule is considerably more demanding, in some instances doubling the volume of the college game.

7) Strength "peaks" as we age (approximately twenty-nine to thirty years). The aging veteran can prolong his or her career by continuing to focus on general strength levels.

8) A good program should encompass each motor ability at varying capacities throughout the year, based on readiness and purposeful planning.

The SSC: Power Implications

The three phases of the SSC are 1) preactivation, 2) short eccentric phase, and 3) immediate transition.

In order to understand how the stretch shortening cycle works, it's imperative to understand how reflex arcs work in the body. A reflex is an involuntary response to a stimulus. The arc is composed of a receptor, an afferent/sensory link, a reflex center, an efferent link, and an effector.[54] In the case of the SSC, the arc is composed of the following components:

- Receptor: muscle spindle
- Afferent link: sensory nerve
- Reflex center: motor control center of brain and CNS
- Efferent link: motor nerve
- Effector: muscle contraction

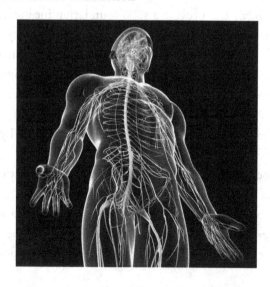

This arc works in a negative feedback loop. A negative feedback loop reads a signal and controls the reaction, preventing injury and homeostatic imbalance. The process begins with an external stimulus—in the case of plyometrics, an aggressive stretch of the soft tissue that signals the muscle spindles (located in the muscle belly) to respond to length changes. Information is sent to the brain via sensory nerves. The brain quickly sends the message via efferent pathways to the muscle to quickly contract to avoid damage. The action of the muscle spindle causing contraction provides negative feedback, protecting the body from potential injury.

Plyometric: pliometric = eccentric contraction
Miometric = concentric contraction

True plyometrics take advantage of the stretch-shortening cycle, using elastic energy stored in the tendons. This is accomplished with minimal transition time (.15 to .20 milliseconds) between eccentric stretch and rapid concentric contraction—in other words, minimal ground contact time! Plyometrics are extremely demanding on the body. It is imperative that the coach has adequate regressions in order to slowly build up to this form of training. Plyometrics are not a first-phase method for most hockey players. The key to power development for hockey players lies in a systemic approach that slowly builds tendon tolerance and rigidity in the system. According to Hooke's law, deformation of the tissue is dependent on its stiffness. Stiffer tissue resists elongation and provides faster recoil.

Hooke's Law

F (restoring force) = k (stiffness) x (deformation distance)

*The goal of jump training and true plyometrics is to increase
the stiffness of the system and produce higher levels of power. In
order to accomplish this goal, a structured program must have
adequate progressions, which act as favorable prerequisites.*

Dr. Mel Siff would call the regressed form of plyometrics power-metrics. During early periods of the preparation block, the goal is to build a solid base of jump mechanics while avoiding high eccentric forces on the athlete. This can be accomplished by jumping onto a box. Single overcoming (no stretch shortening), coupling (eccentric/concentric) jumps, bounds, and hops can all be incorporated. The box is a velocity-friendly mechanism that reduces the impact of the falling weight and the overall load supported during landing. This decreases kinetic energy, making the exercise more user-friendly.

$$E_k = \tfrac{1}{2}mv^2$$

Kinetic Energy = 1/2 (mass x velocity)^2

By landing on a box, we are essentially reducing eccentric forces placed on the athlete during landing. We are reducing the velocity, or the rate of change of distance over time.

Terminology
+ *Jump*—take off on two feet and land on two feet
+ *Hop*—take off on one foot (left foot) and land on one foot (left foot)
+ *Bound*—take off on one foot (left foot) and land on one foot (right foot)

Once tendon tolerance has been built and jumping and landing mechanics are technically proficient, the box can be removed.

Jumping and landing without a box increases eccentric force during impact. During the final three phases, hurdles and minihurdles can be used to increase eccentric demand, thus increasing kinetic energy and taking advantage of elastic recoil. Proper progressions are designed to do the following:

1) Focus on jump mechanics
2) Slowly build eccentric strength and tendon tolerance
3) Introduce an increase in velocity and in eccentric forces
4) Introduce coupling/amortization mechanics, focusing on eccentric/concentric pulses
5) True plyometrics

It's important to have progressions/regressions in program design not just for beginners but also for the desired training effect that you are seeking as a coach (training effect = means (exercise) + methods).

Progressions can be used to load the athlete, to deload the athlete, to taper, or to focus on mechanics. The majority of power training should focus on broadening the base, using power-metrics and various forms of jump training; however, the end goal is the acquisition of this biomotor ability in a well-structured, safe environment.

Methods of Power Development for Hockey Players

Power training is best sequenced immediately after a dynamic warm-up while the athlete is fresh and rested. Three- to five-minute rest periods are necessary for full recovery of the ATP-PC system and the maintenance of proper technique. Density may be built into the workout by alternating between upper- and lower-body power training or by adding corrective work between sets; this is referred to as *active rest*. During the first few phases of jump training, the athlete is instructed to stick the jump and land stiff. This utilizes kinetic energy to deform the supporting tissues. "During soft landing by experienced athletes, only 0.5% of the body's kinetic energy is spent to deform body tissues (bone, cartilage, spine). During a stiff landing, the deformation energy amounts to 75% of the body's mechanical energy. The difference is 150 fold!"[55] Jump training increases the rate of force development; maximizes the muscle action of eccentric, isometric, and concentric contraction; and improves motor unit recruitment and motor unit coordination, all while focusing on improving impulse.

Developing Impulse

The combination of force and time is recognized as impulse. Why is impulse important for hockey players? Hockey players require unique jump training when compared to field-based athletes. On the ice, there is less friction experienced during skating when compared to running. Friction is the force resisting motion on solid surfaces. In addition, foot contact time, because of the length of the skate blade, is considerably longer than in sprinting. This gives the hockey player more time to produce force when compared to his or her sprinting counterpart. Jump training for advanced players should reinforce this concept by creating activity-specific progressions. "Since contraction durations during the skating strides averaged approximately one third of a second (324–387 milliseconds), plyometric training should involve higher amplitude activities resulting in longer ground contact times, ensuring hockey-specific contraction profiles."[56]

$$impulse = force \times \Delta time$$

The Importance of Impulse: Differences between Skating and Sprinting

Skating	Sprinting
Start: V start, start low and stay low	Start: from the blocks, start low, get vertical
Ice surface: less friction	Ground surface: more friction
Impulse: greater impulse (324–387 ms per foot contact)	Impulse: less impulse (90 ms per foot contact)
Acceleration: stride pattern from short to long Shin angle: remains positive and horizontal during stride Acceleration height: the angle you apply force will dictate recovery height; acceleration height is low during acceleration	Acceleration: sprint pattern is long to short Shin angle: changes from horizontal to vertical Acceleration height: much higher in vertical sprinting
Biomechanics: arm swing during acceleration is long, pushing down and back to counter the balance of the lower body	Biomechanics: Max velocity = short arm swing, elbow joint closes

Sprinting: Charlie Francis Speed Zones

Start: 0–10 m
Acceleration: 0–30 m
Max Velocity: 50–80 m (< 8s)
Speed Endurance: 80–150 m (8–15 s)
Special Endurance 1: 150–300 (15–45s)
Special Endurance 2: 300–600 (>45 s)

In a one-hundred-meter race, the majority of acceleration occurs in the first thirty meters. When looking at the various speed zones as it pertains to sprinting, it is apparent that hockey is a game of acceleration and not top-end max velocity. Very rarely do players sprint for eighty-meter puck races. On the contrary, many battles for puck possession are ten feet or less. Acceleration provides longer ground contact time and more time to apply force. Another important concept to remember is that hockey players need to be able to change direction, stop, start, and pivot while maintaining efficiency. In order to do so, a lower center of mass is of primary importance.

Linear/Lateral Power-Metric Box Jumps/Hops

Power-metric box jumps are a great first progression for jump training. Single overcoming (concentric only) or coupling (eccentric/concentric) jumps can be used. Many coaches prefer using overcoming progressions, as this provides greater impulse, comparable to foot contact times as experienced on the ice. Foot contact time on the ice, approximately 387 milliseconds (ms), is four times longer than that experienced by a sprinter (90 milliseconds). Box height is predicated by mechanical mastery. The athlete should jump and land in roughly the same position. If this cannot be accomplished, use a smaller box. The box is a great tool, as it reduces eccentric landing forces and places less overall stress on the system.

Method	Target	Guidelines	Rest	Volume	Frequency
Power-metric box jumps	Increase concentric strength and impulse, focus on mechanics	Explosive	3–5 minutes	3x3–5 (9–15 total jumps)	1–2 sessions/week

Box Jumps

Linear Box Hops

Lateral Box Hops

Linear/Lateral Power-Metric Hurdle Jumps

The next progression in jump training is the removal of the box and the addition of a hurdle or mini hurdle. The athlete will now be introduced to larger impact forces during landing. Again, the athlete is instructed to stick the landing, firmly increasing tension while maintaining the integrity of the system. Hurdle height is chosen based on sound technique and the ability to land in the same anatomical position as on takeoff.

Method	Target	Guidelines	Rest	Volume	Frequency
Power-metric hurdle jumps	Increase eccentric strength/ landing mechanics	Explosive	3–5 minutes	3x3–5 (9–15 total jumps)	1–2 sessions/week

Hurdle Jumps

Lateral Hurdle Hops

Hurdle jumps are introduced gradually, as this increases eccentric strain on the athlete. Jumping mechanics do not change.

(Lateral Bounds: Lateral bounds are also a fantastic way to increase eccentric load while maximizing foot contact in a horizontal manner.)

Loaded Jumps

Loaded jumps are used as a tool to increase power output and impulse. Loads of 10 to 20 percent 1RM (one repetition maximum) typically constitute appropriate load under tension while jumping. As Vladimir Zatsiorsky states: "The ability to produce maximal force and the ability to achieve great velocity in the same motion are different motor abilities. Maximal power is achieved in the intermediate range of force and velocity."[57] Jumps can be loaded by incorporating different tools, such as kettle bells, dumbbells, trap bars, or barbells.

Method	Target	Guidelines	Rest	Volume	Frequency
Loaded jumps	Producing force under external load	10–20% of 1 RM	3–5 minutes	3x3–5 (9–15 total jumps)	1–2 sessions/week

Loaded Jumps

Loaded Squat Jump—The athlete attains triple extension of the ankles, knees, and hips and lands in the same position he or she started in.

Developing Amortization Mechanics

Linear/Lateral Power-Metric Pulses

The amortization phase, or switching phase, is a short period between eccentric and concentric contraction. A shorter period leads to less ground contact time, thus a more explosive athlete. The athlete jumps, hops, or bounds over a hurdle and upon landing executes a quick pulse (eccentric to concentric contraction) before moving on to the next jump. Hurdle height is chosen based on minimal ground contact time.

Method	Target	Guidelines	Rest	Volume	Frequency
Power-metric hurdle jumps w/ amortization	Decrease time between eccentric/ concentric contractions	Explosive	3–5 minutes	3x3–5 (9–15 total jumps)	1–2 sessions/week

True Plyometrics

Continuous jumps, hops, or bounds with minimal ground contact time constitute true plyometric training. This method is demanding on the entire system because it is both high velocity and high load to the system. It is imperative that a young athlete slowly builds up to plyometric training.

Box/hurdle height is chosen based on landing technique and ground contact time. As the late, great sprint coach Charlie Francis states, "The best plyo drills for speed are vertical in nature, i.e., hurdle hops or hops initiated from a slight height, but stay below thirty inches. Anything higher will kill the elastic response you're looking for."

Method	Target	Guidelines	Rest	Volume	Frequency
True plyometrics	Minimal ground contact time (15–20 seconds)	Explosive	3–5 minutes	3x3–5 (9–15 total jumps)	1–2 sessions/week

Upper-Body Med Ball Throws

Upper-body med ball throws link the entire kinetic chain: feet, ankles, hips, spine, and hands during dynamic, explosive movement. During throws, the athlete is able to accelerate the ball through a full range of motion without neuromuscular inhibition. This is not the case with traditional resistance training, as the nervous system decelerates the movement at end-range to spare stress and torque on the system.

Method	Target	Guidelines	Rest	Volume	Frequency
Upper-body throws	Upper-body power	Explosive	3–5 minutes	3x3–5 (9–15 total throws)	1–2 sessions/week

Kneeling MB throw w/ Hip Extension

Half-kneeling MB throw

Standing MB throw w/ Extension

Kneeling MB side throw

Half-kneeling MB side throw

Standing MB side throw

Additional Methods

Speed strength is the ability to produce force under high velocity, moderate load, or speed in the presence of strength.

Olympic Lifting

Teaching variations of the Olympic lifts is a debatable topic in the field of hockey strength and conditioning. These lifts take years to master and take considerable time to teach. In addition, some coaches would argue that the range of motion of these lifts isn't specific enough to meet the demands of hockey. Hockey is a hip-flexed sport with extension of the ankles and knees; power is generated in a predominately horizontal direction, although vertical foce production is a necessity as well. Some coaches might omit Olympic lifts in favor of loaded jumps.

Other coaches favor Olympic lifting variations for the reasons mentioned here.

- Axial/anteroposterior-loaded movement
- Taxes the entire kinetic chain
- Teaches the athlete how to produce force effectively
- Enhances fast-twitch (white fiber) capacity
- Ingrains complex motor programs in the CNS
- CNS-intensive exercise
- Teaches the athlete how to absorb force effectively

In the author's opinion, teaching the Olympic lifts from the hang position is superior for the hockey-playing population. This is a more specific position relative to the sport and much less technical to teach. Loads should alternate between 65 to 75 percent for repetitions of three to five and 80 to 85 percent for repetitions of two to three.

Power Clean from the Hang: Starting Position
1. Slight knee bend, approximately 120 to 130 degrees.
2. Bar placed above the knee in the hang position.
3. Elbows externally rotated with shoulders slightly ahead of the bar.
4. Extend the ankles, knees, and hips.
5. Drive your elbows "through the mirror."

Method	Target	Guidelines	Rest	Volume	Frequency
Olympic lifting	Full-body intermuscular coordination	Explosive	1–3 minutes	3x1x5 (3–15 total reps)	1–2 sessions/week

Contrast Method

The *contrast method* (also known as complex training) is a potentiation tool utilized to enhance the athlete's rate of force development. Complex training involves performing a heavy compound movement, followed by plyometric movement of a similar pattern. This creates a postactivation potentiation, or PAP. This means that a more powerful muscular action may be achieved if it is preceded by a strong muscular contraction facilitating high-threshold motor units.

Method	Target	Guidelines	Rest	Volume	Frequency
Complex method	Heavy compound exercise (80–90% of 1RM), followed by an explosive plyometric or strength-based exercise	Explosive	3–5 minutes	3x3–5 (9–15 total reps)	1–2 sessions/week

Day 1	Tempo	Rest	WK1	G: +/-/=	Reps	WK 2	G: +/-/+=	Reps	WK 3	G: +/-/+=	Reps	WK 4	G:+/-/+=	Reps
A1.) Trap Bar DL w/chains	(1/0/0)	3min			x5			x3			x3			x3
OR Deadlift	(1/0/0)	3min			x5			x3			x3			x3
								x3			x3			x3
A2.) Power Clean	Explosive	3 min			x3			x2			x2			x2
	Explosive	3 min			x3			x2			x2			x2
								x2			x2			x2
A3.) Trap Bar Jumps (15-20%)		3 min			x10			x10			x10			x10
		3 min			x10			x10			x10			x10
					x10			x10			x10			x10
A4.) Depth Jumps		3 min			x10			x10			x10			x10
		3 min			x10			x10			x10			x10
					x10			x10			x10			x10
A5.) Vertical Jump		3 min			:15			:15			:15			:15
		3 min			:15			:15			:15			:15
		3 min			:15			:15			:15			:15

An example of a Bulgarian complex used to create postactivation potentiation. Maximal strength is attacked first, recruiting high-threshold motor units in order to increase power output in the more ballistic movements that proceed.

Review

Power training is essential in the development of the complete hockey player. Like all other biomotor abilities, power is dependent on adequate levels of maximum strength. In order to increase the rate of force development, adequate force must already exist. If this is not the case, spending time on the left side of the force velocity curve may exploit these imbalances and create a solid foundation for future power gains. Most power exercises are deliberately programmed at the onset of exercise protocol, keeping the central nervous system fresh and stimulated while limiting the residual fatigue and technical breakdown accompanied by prolonged work. Power training serves to increase conduction velocity of muscle contraction while increasing motor unit recruitment, rate coding (firing rates), and synchronization. These qualities transfer onto the ice in the form of increased speed, acceleration, and shooting velocity.

Proper progressions enable athletes from all training backgrounds to safely engage in plyometric training. By understanding the components, we can properly design appropriate progressions.

Breaking Down Plyometrics

Yielding Phase
- Eccentric contraction
- Landing
- Rapid muscle lengthening
- Triple flexion

Coupling Phase
- Switching phase
- Eccentric to concentric
- Flexion to extension
- Explosive stretch to explosive contraction

Overcoming Phase
- Concentric contraction
- Takeoff
- Rapid muscle shortening
- Triple extension

To build jump/plyometric progressions, simply reverse-engineer the process. The key is to slowly move from simple to complex, minimal force acceptance/output to maximal force acceptance/output. The following continuum moves from minimal eccentric demand on the system to maximal demand and seeks to organize the appropriate progressions:

1) Learn to slow down and apply the brakes while minimizing eccentric forces.
2) Teach jump technique with minimal force acceptance during impact.
3) Slowly add eccentric demand via introducing hurldes.
4) Use long to short coupling while increasing eccentric demands. Keep in mind that some coaches do not use short coupling times with hockey players because long-amplitude jumps are more appropriate to the impulse experienced on the ice.
5) Use repeated stretching/contraction, sharp yielding and overcoming.

Eccentric Demands: Breaking Down the Components of Plyometric Training

Low Demand		High Demand
Long Coupling Time		Minimal Coupling Time

←--→

| Overcoming Phase | Coupling Phase | Yielding Phase |

Exercises

Box jumps	Jump stick/jump pulse	Plyometrics
Hurdle jump	Linear/lateral hops w/pulse	Depth jumps
Squat jump		

Progression #1—Overcoming Phase (Minimize Eccentric Demand)

Manipulating the kinetic energy equation and decreasing eccentric forces will seek to increase tendon tolerance while building rigidity of the system, enabling the athlete to accept larger loads at higher velocities. Early in the training process is a great time to focus on jump mechanics and the intricacies of takeoff and landing. This is accomplished by jumping (concentric contraction) onto a box (decreases eccentric forces).

Progression #2—Yielding/Long Coupling Phase (Moderate Eccentric Demand)

Removing the box and jumping over an object (e.g., hurdles) increases eccentric forces, placing greater physical demands on the athlete. This can also be accomplished with a loaded jump squat. Longer coupling times can aid the athlete in accepting greater loads safely, while maintaining technical proficiency. There is also a strong carryover onto the ice; long amplitude jumps provide great transfer relevant to the demands of the hockey stride. Long to short coupling times can be accomplished with jump-stick protocol or the addition of elastic pulses between landing and takeoff. Coupling seeks to build on tendon tolerance while increasing the demands of conduction velocity of the neuromuscular apparatus.

Progression #3—Sharp Yielding/Short Coupling (Maximal Eccentric Demand)

Although all progressions have eccentric components, the greatest demands are experienced during minimal ground contact time in the presence of repeated stretching and contraction. As coupling times decrease and velocity increases, appropriate tendon stiffness is needed to increase performance and decrease the chance of soft-tissue injury. Eccentric forces are highest during true plyometrics, and the tendons and corresponding connective tissue need to be prepared to accept these large forces. A sharp yielding phase immediately followed by a strong concentric contraction is the key to taking advantage of kinetic energy stored in the system. Strength coaches should keep in mind that hockey players and field sports athletes have different needs. Ground contact times, impulse, and friction are very different. Many coaches avoid true plyometrics for hockey players and instead focus on high-amplitude, long-impulse jump training, as these modalities focus more on providing appropriate impulse at the expense of the SSC. "Since contraction durations during the skating strides averaged approximately one third of a second (324–387 milliseconds), plyometric training should involve higher amplitude activities resulting in longer ground contact times, ensuring hockey-specific contraction profiles."[58]

SSC (reactive strength) is dependent on the following:
- Training age
- Time of year
- Footwear
- Flooring / playing surface
- Fiber type
- Tendon tolerance—stiffer tissue stretches less and provides faster recoil
- Supporting musculature of the kinetic chain
- Maximal strength levels
- Velocity during eccentric phase
- Short amortization phase
- Sharp elastic recoil

Potential Off-Season Power Periodization Scheme for Hockey Players

POWER DEVELOPMENT

	Days 1 and 3 (Linear)	Days 2 and 4 (Lateral)
Phase 1	Upper Body: Kneeling MB Throw w/hip ext 3x5 Lower Body: Box Jumps 3x5	Upper Body: Kneeling MB Side Throw 3x5 Lower Body: Lateral Box Hops 3x6
Phase 2	Upper Body: Half Kneeling MB Throw 3x5 Lower Body: Hurdle Jumps 3x5	Upper Body: Half Kneeling MB Side Throw 3x5 Lower Body: Lateral Hurdle Hops 3x6
Phase 3	Upper Body: Standing MB Throw w/ext 3x5 Lower Body: Squat Jumps w/stick 3x5	Upper Body: Standing MB Side Throw 3x5 Lower Body: 45 degree bounds 3x6
Phase 4	Upper Body: Approaching MB Throw 3x5 Lower Body: Explosive Squat Jumps 3x5	Upper Body: Approaching MB Side Throw 3x5 Lower Body: Continuous 45 degree bounds 3x6

Chapter 6

Acceleration

For me, the most important phase in sprinting is the
acceleration phase. This is mainly because it is the longest
phase and is also easily trainable, since it is here that the
explosive strength of the athlete expresses itself best.

If is also the phase in which adequate strength training can make a big
difference, contrary to reaction time, block start, or maximum speed.
—Henk Kraaijenhof

The hockey player faces an entirely different objective than his or her
sprinting counterpart. In the sprinting disciplines, the goal is to get vertical
and sustain max velocity. In the sport of hockey, max velocity is rarely,
if ever, recognized, and getting vertical proves to be a disadvantageous,
noneconomical position. Hockey is a game of acceleration, not top-end
speed. The majority of acceleration occurs between zero and thirty meters
in a one-hundred-meter sprint. In the game of hockey, puck races are ten
to fifteen feet in length and rely on the ability of the athlete to accelerate.

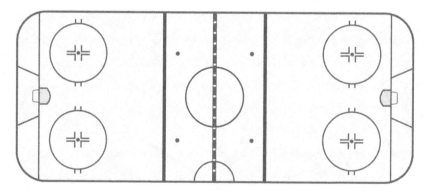

The dimensions of a regulation-sized ice surface are two hundred by eighty-five feet. Most puck races in the game of hockey take place in tight, confined quarters. Very rarely do players engage in thirty- or more meter (over ninety-foot) efforts. Acceleration is a key component in building the complete hockey player.

In order to accelerate the proper biomechanical considerations must be accounted for:

+ Deep knee bend
+ Positive shin angle
+ Horizontal displacement
+ Complete line of extension from shoulders to ankle
+ High relative strength to overcome inertia and initiate propulsion
+ Acceleration led by the arms (The arms are closer in proximity to the brain's motor cortex than the legs.)
+ Long arm swing, pushing down and back to counter the balance of the lower body
+ Arms reaching chin level during front side mechanics and clearing the hips during back side mechanics

Ground contact times are much longer during acceleration than in top-end sprinting, thus placing more importance on relative strength measures (the athlete's strength relative to his or her body weight). Increasing strength gains in the weight room may have a direct correlation into improvements in acceleration, but this must not be the only means of attempting to increase this biomotor ability. Starting strength (generating force at the onset of muscle contraction) and acceleration strength (time to max force) are time dependent, whereas maximal strength is not. As strength/sprint coach James Smith states,

> More force equals more acceleration! This would result in the idea that simply getting an athlete stronger, provided body mass is constant, will result in increased acceleration ability. This is an incomplete notion. We must account for the fact that time is of the essence. During early acceleration ground contact times (CGT) are longer, and longer CGT provides more time to apply force. As speed increases more

force is generated at ground contact; however, as the speed increases there is less time to apply force.[59]

There is no weight-training activity that can mimic the limited time the ankle/foot complex has to produce force in both the sprinting and on-ice disciplines. Absolute strength in the weight room is not dependent on time; acceleration and speed rely on it!

There are several ways to improve acceleration ability for the competitive hockey player. For the youth player, simply increasing range of motion, intermuscular coordination, and relative/absolute strength may be the best means of accomplishing this task. Absolute strength is paramount for the growing athlete. Without adequate levels of strength, acceleration and speed may be compromised. In order to display strength as quickly as possible, adequate levels of strength must already exist. A well-programmed strength and conditioning plan may work wonders, creating an immediate improvement in acceleration ability. In addition, skating may be considered a high forward speed but slowly performed movement. As expert coach Frans Bosch states, "In slow sporting movements, the intramuscular demands on muscles are not as extreme as during high-speed movements. The problem with slow sporting movements is far more the way in which intermuscular coordination is linked to body posture during movement."[60] This places a high degree of importance on coordinative, multijoint movements that challenge the system and build coordination. Exercises, such as Olympic lifts and loaded jumps, may fit in this category. Finally plyometrics play a crucial role in building requisite tendon tolerance, as the force/time profiles are much more similar to those expressed during acceleration on the ice. Both plyometric training and adequate strength serve as a foundational means of initially improving acceleration.

Linear and lateral acceleration drills may also be incorporated into the program prior to weight training and placed before jump training. Exercise means that have a high-contraction velocity should take place when the nervous system is fresh and ready to express high levels of coordinated force. When designing acceleration drills, the coach should build adequate progressions based on the level of difficulty and the biomechanical aspects of the sport. In addition, distance should be kept short, which makes the endeavor a more knee-dominant exercise, eliminating the hamstring complex as a decelerator of terminal knee extension during top-end speed. The following are several progressions of both linear and lateral acceleration drills for hockey players.

Prone Linear Push-Up Start—A lower center of mass is more advantageous for overcoming inertia in a horizontal direction. Athletes who are not as powerful will benefit from a greater departure angle.

Linear Half-Kneeling Start

2-Pt Start

Linear Sled Sprint

In addition to these drills, hill sprinting is a fantastic way to build acceleration during the off-season for the competitive hockey player. Running uphill mimics the contact pattern of the skate, as more of the foot makes contact with the ground. This increases impulse. "In uphill running the drop height per step is reduced, and therefore so is the amount of kinetic energy that can be converted. Muscle action will therefore shift from isometric (elastic) to concentric, and energy costs will increase."[61] Uphill running for five to ten seconds with approximately fifty-five to sixty seconds of rest is an excellent way to focus on acceleration ability while taxing the alactic system.

Half-Kneeling Lateral Start—Note how the inside leg (right) is the push leg for forward and defensemen, while the outside leg (left) is the pull leg. This is much different for goaltenders and field-based athletes. Goaltenders and field-based athletes would set up with the left leg up. It would assume the responsibility of the push leg, while the right leg was the pull leg. Mechanics change based on the surface (ice versus ground), footwear (skates versus running shoes), and positional demands (forward versus goaltenders versus field-based athletes).

Powerful COD/acceleration is accomplished with a push from the inside leg and a pull from the outside leg respectively.

Lateral Band Cross-Under Step

Lateral Short Stop Starts—Note how the athlete crosses under and pushes with the inside leg. This progression would be appropriate for forward and defensemen.

Lateral Short Stop Starts—Note how the athlete pushes with the outside leg. This progression would be appropriate for goaltenders.

Final thoughts on Acceleration

F = m x a (force = mass x acceleration); therefore a = f/m (acceleration = force/mass)

If mass remains constant, increasing force will have tangible effects on acceleration. If force remains constant and mass increases, acceleration may be altered negatively. Get strong first! The best means of increasing acceleration ability in the growing player is to build an adequate base of absolute strength. Time-dependent motor abilities should be incorporated into a strength and conditioning plan. Jump training, short acceleration exercises, hill sprints, and sled work all fit into this category. As speed increases, the amount of time we have to display our strength decreases. Train fast!

Intermuscular coordination is another important variable in displaying fast forward movement with relatively slower contraction velocities as compared to sprinting. Coordination under load is important. Olympic lifts, multijoint lifts, and sensory challenges while under mechanical load may be incorporated into a program to train this ability.

Potential Off-Season Acceleration Periodization
Scheme for Hockey Players

ACCELERATION

	Days 1 and 3 (Linear)	Days 2 and 4 (Lateral)
Phase 1	Push-Up Starts x5 (1:00 rest in between) 1:00 rest between reps	Lateral Push Up Starts x5 1:00 rest bewteen reps
Phase 2	Half Kneeling Start x5 1:00 rest between reps	Half Kneeling Lateral Start (Inside Leg Push) x5 1:00 rest between reps
Phase 3	2-Pt Start x5 1:00 rest between reps	Short Stop Start (Inside leg pushes) x5 1:00 rest between reps
Phase 4	2-Pt Start w/tennis ball drop x5 1:00 rest between reps	Short Stop Start w/tennis ball drop x5 1:00 rest between reps

Chapter 7

Strength and Conditioning

I believe that strength training does not need to be as specific to
the sporting action as some suggest. Speed training needs to have a
greater degree of specificity than strength training, and the energy
system training has the greatest need of all three for specificity.
—Ian King

Strength is the ability to express force.

General <---> Specific
Strength Training   Speed Training   Endurance Training

Hockey Specific

Train the athlete not the sport.

Strength and conditioning practitioners need to be sound proponents of
general physical preparation in the weight room. There are certain abilities
that cannot be overloaded on the ice; strength is one of these biomotor abilities.
Ill attempts to mimic the demands of hockey while under considerable load
may lead to more harm than good. As Mel Siff states, "This can lead to
the development of inappropriate and conflicting neural programs in the
athlete, because simulation with significant extra loading changes the center
of gravity, torque, acceleration, involvement of elastic energy processes and
patterns of force production." [67] The late, great sprint coach Charlie Francis
echoed these thoughts with regards to weight training implications and the
power conversion phase for elite sprinters. He states, "I also eliminated the
traditional 'conversion phase' which sprint coaches had adopted to bring
velocities in weight-lifting closer to the sprint speed. I concluded that sprinters'
extremities moved so much faster in running than in lifting that any increase
in lifting speed was irrelevant." This may be true for hockey players as well, as

velocities on the ice may reach upward of thirty miles per hour, much greater than those experienced in the weight room while under load.

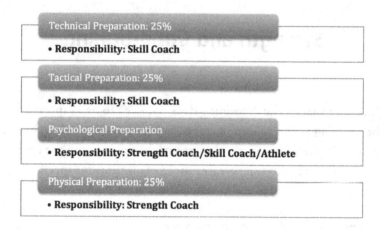

Good strength and conditioning programs are built around the concept of training the athlete, not the sport. Skill coaches are responsible for technical and tactical preparation, while the strength and conditioning practitioner is responsible for physical preparation and to a certain extent for psychological readiness. Physical preparation is at most 25 percent (or one of four components) of athletic success.[62]

General principles of training allow the strength and conditioning coach to structure a program that meets the needs of the individual and the physiology of the sport, while understanding the basic biological pillars that create a foundation for the implementation of future means and methods.

Basic Principles of Training

Methods are many; principles are few.

- *The Principle of Specificity*

    This principle states that adaptation and its desired effect is specific to the individual athlete. No two people are the same; therefore, a program may have differing effects based on body type, training age, psychological maturation, and cumulative stress levels. Adaptation is also specific to the biomechanics, neuromusculature action, and energy system demands of training. Therefore, the closer these stresses are to sport, the greater the transfer of training.

□ *The Principle of Overload*

In order to improve a desired training effect, the stressor must be great enough to solicit a disruption and change in baseline homeostatic levels (i.e., the stimulus must create a stress response). If the stimulus is not great enough to warrant this disruption, strength gains may be jeopardized. Hans Selye's *General Adaptation Syndrome* (1936) states the body will respond to any external stress with a predictable pattern in an attempt to restore homeostasis. If we do not trip the homeostatic wire, we will not get stronger in the weight room. For young athletes, this equates to a progressive resistance program where small increases in weight over time lead to increased strength gains. This is a more difficult task for the advanced athlete. As training age increases, gains are more difficult to attain as the athlete becomes desensitized to the repetition and frequency of the stimulus. As Marty Gallagher states, "Progress is difficult to generate, tough to progress and sure to end." Overload is accomplished through various combinations of volume and intensity. Overload can be programmed by the following:

- Increasing load
- Increasing volume
- Increasing ROM
- Adding variety
- Increasing density
- Altering work-to-rest ratios
- Changing leverage and mechanical advantage
- Changing the base of support (bilateral versus unilateral)

□ *The Principle of Reversibility*

When the training stimulus is taken away or reduced (e.g., intensity, frequency, and density), the adaptation will decrease and gradually weaken. The principle of reversibility works in opposition to the principle of overload. Lack of stimulus leads to maintenance, lack of growth, or atrophy. This can lead to a detraining effect. Fitness benefits can be completely lost after four to eight weeks of detraining.[63]

Basic training principles set the platform and foundation for the creation and establishment of general programming parameters. These principles work hand in hand with the five principles of athletic-based programming. Both elements are crucial in program design and work in a reciprocal fashion, creating athlete-centric programs. The five keys to implementing a physical preparation plan for hockey players are listed here.

Athletic Based Programming

Basic Prinipals of Training

The Five Principles of Athletic-Based Program Design

An amateur marries methods and experiments with principles.
The expert marries principles and experiments with methods.
—Anthony Donskov

All athletic-based principles of program design are created around a single philosophy respected among the strength and conditioning community: do no harm! Ian King states, "The only sports where barbell weight equates to scoreboard success are the weight lifting sports (powerlifting and Olympic lifting)." These are sports where weight on the bar is lifted in attempt to break a record or win a competition. One cannot train a sport with a sport or hold the standards of one sport to the training demands of another. Power lifting, Olympic lifting, and bodybuilding are sports. The demands of these sports are very different than the demands of hockey. Variations of these strength-based sports may be used to design an effective athletic-based program, but not one single form of training should constitute an entire plan. Athletic-based training for team and individual sport is a unique blend of biomotor abilities, such as strength, power, capacity, acceleration, change of direction, and speed. Although the goal is to increase weight on the bar and get stronger, weight should never compromise the athlete's safety or technical elements of the lift. The sport of hockey is played on the ice, not in the weight room. The goal is to build strong, powerful, and healthy players, ready for the demands of a long, grueling hockey season. It is better to have a player front squat three hundred pounds and play every game of the season than a player who can front squat four hundred pounds but misses half the season with a stress fracture in his lower back from being too aggressive in the weight room. It is form that dictates weight on the bar, and the coach's responsibility is maintaining safety.

Strength Coach Rule #1: Do No Harm
- Eliminate injury in the weight room.
- Reduce avoidable soft-tissue injuries on the ice.
- Enhance performance.

Principle 1: Train Movement Patterns

Movement before volume, volume before strength.
—Dan John

If you train patterns, you will not miss muscles. If you train muscles, you will miss patterns.
—Team Exos

Isolation does not equal integration; the body functions as a unit. Each interdependent system functions to maintain homeostasis and provide systemic balance. All muscles work synergistically. During the demands of hockey, the body works as one functional unit with agonists, antagonists, and synergists all working together to contract, stabilize, and provide structural support eccentrically, isometrically, and concentrically. Isolating joint segments and range of motion does not prepare the nervous system to work interdependently and thus does not properly prepare the hockey player for the demands of the sport.

An example of an isolated exercise is the leg extension used in both rehab and strength and conditioning settings. Leg extensions prevent the hip from sharing load and places undue stress on the knee joint. In addition, leg extensions prevent the nervous system from recruiting muscle synergists to perform complex patterns and nullify the use of the prestretch prior to initiating movement. This compromises the system and joint structure, as now the prescribed exercise initiates at the weakest mechanical point.

Movement can be divided into six basic patterns. These patterns play an integral role in creating balanced programs designed to build symmetry while avoiding muscle imbalance. In addition, these patterns recruit the entire CNS and respective muscle stabilizers/synergists. Coaches may bucket these patterns into the following categories:

Horizontal Push	Horizontal Pull	Vertical Pull	Vertical Push	Knee Dominant	Hip Dominant

Once these patterns have been established, coaches can strategically begin to build an exercise library, creating a database of effective exercise protocol based around the concept of integration versus isolation. In addition to categorizing and creating an exercise log, coaches can further break down exercises into foundational versus accessory lifts. Foundational lifts (bolded) are the bedrock patterns for sports performance and comprise large, multijoint, compound lifts that are the staple of programming for strength and conditioning professionals (bang for your buck). Accessory lifts serve to complement foundational lifts and aid in further strengthening of the surrounding musculature and any weak points within the specified pattern. The best accessory exercise for a particular lift is one that most closely resembles the lift itself.

Horizontal Push	Horizontal Pull	Vertical Pull	Vertical Push	Knee Dominant	Hip Dominant
Bench press	DB row	Wide grip chin up	Barbell OH press	Back squat	Dead lift
Incline bench press	BB row	Neutral grip chin up	Standing OH DB press	Front squat	Trap bar DL
DB bench press	TRX row	Sternum pull ups	Standing DB alt. OH press	RFESS	SLDL
Incline DB bench press	Single arm TRX pull	Lat pull down	Single arm OH press	Split squat	RDL
	X-pull			Goblet squat	Reverse lunge
	Face pull				Loaded hip lift
					SB leg curl

Movement Pattern Library—Coaches can begin to "bucket" patterns, creating an exercise menu of available means. In addition, exercises can be further divided into foundational lifts and accessory lifts.

Balancing Patterns

All things being equal, and independent of any specificity demands, the selection of exercises should show balance throughout the body.
—Ian King

The goal for the strength and conditioning practitioner is to create a program that establishes balance. Balance is obtained when patterns are paired and sequenced in order to create a cause-and-effect relationship. Cause and effect builds symmetry through balancing out the six movement patterns. When writing programs for athletes, all patterns should be incorporated during a weekly microcycle and balanced based on the frequency of training. The order of sequences can be manipulated each block (three to six weeks) to prioritize movement, or additional volume can be added to certain patterns to reverse any preexisting musculoskeletal imbalances.

Cause and Effect

Horizontal Push <----------> Horizontal Pull

*Horizontal pushing anteriorly tips the scapula;
horizontal pulling posteriorly tips the scapula.*

Vertical Push <----------------> Vertical Pull

*Vertical pushing increases humeral head migration;
vertical pulling decreases humeral head migration.*

Knee Dominant <-------------> Hip Dominant

*Knee dominance anteriorly rotates the pelvis; hip dominance
posteriorly rotates the pelvis*

Frequency-Based Cause and Effect: Two-Day-per-Week Programming

Program Design: Movement

<u>2 Day Per Week Program: Full Body</u>

 Day 1

A1.) Knee Dominant
A2.) Horizontal Push
A3.) Vertical Pull

B1.) Hip Dominant
B2.) Horizontal Pull
B3.) Vertical Push

 Day 2

A1.) Hip Dominant
A2.) Horizontal Pull
A3.) Vertical Push

B1.) Knee Dominant
B2.) Horizontal Push
B3.) Vertical Pull

Sample: Two-Day-per-Week Full Body Program

*All movement buckets are accounted for, breaking the
training up into two manageable full-body workouts.*

Progra m Design

2 Day Per Week Program: Knee Dominant/Hip Dominant

 Day 1   **Day 2**

Day 1	Day 2
A1.) Knee Dominant	A1.) Hip Dominant
A2.) Horizontal Push	A2.) Vertical Push
B1.) Knee Dominant	B1.) Hip Dominant
B2.) Horizontal Pull	B2.) Vertical Pull
B3.) Core	B3.) Core

Sample: Two-Day-per-Week Knee-Dominant/Hip-Dominant Program

All movement buckets are accounted for, breaking the training week up into a knee-dominant day while focusing on horizontal patterning and a hip-dominant day, focusing on vertical patterning. This is a great option if the training schedule does not allow for twenty-four to forty-eight hours of recovery.

Progra m Design

2 Day Per Week Program: Knee Dominant: Push/Hip Dominant: Pull

 Day 1   **Day 2**

Day 1	Day 2
A1.) Knee Dominant	A1.) Hip Dominant
A2.) Horizontal Push	A2.) Vertical Pull
B1.) Knee Dominant	B1.) Hip Dominant
B2.) Vertical Push	B2.) Horizontal Pull
B3.) Core	B3.) Core

Sample: Two-Day-per-Week Knee-Dominant/Hip-Dominant Program

All movement buckets are accounted for, breaking the training week up into a knee-dominant day while focusing on pushing patterns and a hip-dominant day, focusing on pulling patterns. This breakdown taxes the anterior kinetic chain on day 1 while focusing on the posterior kinetic chain on day 2.

Frequency-Based Cause and Effect: Four-Day-per-Week Programming

4 Day Per Week Program

Day 1	Day 2	Day 3	Day 4
A1.) Olympic Lift	A1.) Horizontal Push	A1.) Olympic Lift	A1.) Horizontal Push
A2.) Corrective Stretch	A2.) Corrective Pull	A2.) Corrective Stretch	A2.) Corrective Pull
B1.) Knee Dominant	A3.) Core	B1.) Hip Dominant	A3.) Core
B2.) Vertical Pull	B1.) Vertical Push	B2.) Vertical Pull	B1.) Vertical Pull
B3.) Core	B2.) Corrective Stretch	B3.) Core	B2.) Corrective Stretch
C1.) Hip Dominant	B3.) Core	C1.) Knee Dominant	B3.) Core
C2.) Horizontal Pull		C2.) Horizontal Pull	
C3.) Core		C3.) Core	

Sample: Four-Day-per-Week Split (Lower: Pull; Upper: Push)

All movement buckets are accounted for, breaking the training week up into a lower-body pull day and an upper-body push day. Adding the upper-body pulling patterns during the traditional lower-body day builds density into the program.

4 Day Per Week Program

Day 1	Day 2	Day 3	Day 4
A1.) Olympic Lift	A1.) Horizontal Push	A1.) Olympic Lift	A1.) Horizontal Pull
A2.) Corrective Stretch	A2.) Corrective Stretch	A2.) Corrective Stretch	A2.) Corrective Stretch
B1.) Knee Dominant	A3.) Core	B1.) Hip Dominant	A3.) Core
B2.) Vertical Pull	B1.) Horizontal Pull	B2.) Vertical Push	B1.) Horizontal Push
B3.) Core	B2.) Corrective Stretch	B3.) Core	B2.) Corrective Stretch
C1.) Knee Dominant	B3.) Core	C1.) Hip Dominant	B3.) Core
C2.) Vertical Pull		C2.) Vertical Push	
C3.) Core		C3.) Core	

Sample: Four-Day-per-Week Split (Lower: Pull; Upper: Push)

All movement buckets are accounted for, breaking the training week up into one knee-dominant day with vertical pulling and

one hip-dominant day with vertical pushing. The remaining
days (day 2 and day 4) are upper-body push and pull.

Principle 2: Big Rocks

Never eat dessert (isolation exercises) before the meat and potatoes
(compound exercises) and if you are full, skip the dessert.
—Marty Gallagher

This programming variable is based on the Pareto principle, a.k.a.
the 80/20 rule. When designing strength and conditioning programs
for athletes, 20 percent of your exercise protocol will produce 80 percent
of your results. The 20 percent consists of large, multijoint lifts that tax
the entire nervous system. Each of the six patterns listed should have at
least one of these foundational lifts, which form the bedrock for athletic-
based programming. Generally these are barbell lifts that incorporate a
large amount of intermuscular coordination and large groups of muscle
synergists that work together to execute the desired pattern. These lifts may
be manipulated each block (three to six weeks) but remain in some form or
another in the developmental plan during the yearly training cycle. These
lifts are sequenced as prioritized patterns that are performed at the onset
of a program while the athlete is in a recovered state and the CNS is fresh.
Modification of base techniques, such as bar placement, foot positioning,
grip, range of motion, tempo, and recovery are all variables that can be
manipulated while performing and programming these lifts. In addition,
the orthopedics of the athlete warrant strong consideration when designing
programs and choosing foundational lifts. Fit the program to the athlete,
not the athlete to the program. Previous injury, lack of movement base,
and inefficient stability all play a role in choosing the appropriate means of
athletic development. When choosing foundational lifts to incorporate into
athletic-based programming, Coach Dan John recommends answering the
following questions.

+ What are the three to five most important keys to success in the
  sport being trained?

+ What are the most important elements needed to attain these keys that can be trained in the weight room?

+ What does the athlete currently lack?

Building a Foundation: Athletic-Based Big Rocks

Horizontal Push	Horizontal Pull	Vertical Pull	Vertical Push	Knee Dominant	Hip Dominant
Bench press	DB row	Chin-up	DB OH press	Back squat	Dead lift
Incline bench	BB row	Wide grip chin-up	KB BU OH press	Front squat	Trap bar DL
				RFESS	SLDL
				SL Squat	

Foundational lifts are the 20 percent of the exercise protocol that produces 80 percent of athletic development in the weight room. These exercises should be prioritized in programming and sequenced at the onset of strength training while the athlete is fresh and rested.

Principle 3: Periodization

Periodization is a daily concept—be ready to adjust.
—Patrick Ward

Periodization is a concept, not a rigid model. Periodization breaks the training process into manageable periods. It is a concept that supports the idea that *peak condition* is not attainable on a year-round basis. Periodization allows practitioners to structure ebbs and flows into the training process and create "peaks" so that the athletes may realize their gains. The need for structured recovery and regeneration are important as well. Periodization creates balance and structured sequence in athletic-based programming. These manageable periods can be broken down further into blocks or phases of training.

+ Microcycle—one week of training

+ Mesocycle—the linking of four to six microcycles (Think of this as a block of training.)
+ Macrocycle—the linking of two or more mesocycles (Think of this as a training cycle.)

Let the micro dictate the macro.

> We know the most about a plan when we are
> deep in the process, *not* months before.
> —Stuart McMillian

"Modern theory of periodization was originally advanced by L. P. Matveyev (USSR), as an updating of his work, which he first introduced in 1962. Matveyev suggested that the year be divided into 3 categories: preparation (adaptation), competition (application) and transition (regeneration)."[64] When creating a periodized plan for hockey players, the season schedule will heavily influence the amount of time each athlete will spend in the respective categories or blocks of training. A general breakdown of each phase is shown here.

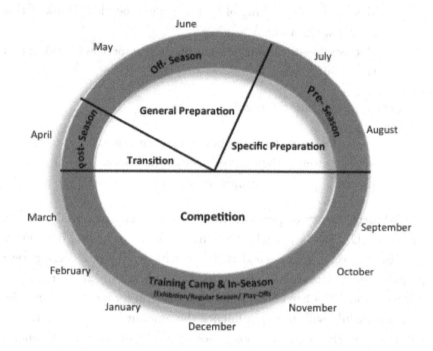

Transition
+ Time frame: April (+/- two weeks)
+ Biomotor abilities trained: active recovery, circuit training, aerobic capacity.

General Preparation (Off-Season)
+ Time frame: May/June
+ Biomotor abilities trained: general accumulation of strength, aerobic capacity with conversion to aerobic power, alactic power with conversion to alactic capacity, flexibility, increase general physical preparation

Specific Preparation (Off-Season)
+ Time frame: July/August
+ Biomotor abilities trained: max strength with conversion to strength endurance or power, lactate power with a conversion to lactate capacity, and short-term aerobic miniblocks to sustain aerobic gains

Please note that during anaerobic development, power is trained prior to capacity. First, athletes need to train for speed. By gaining speed, an athlete can gradually increase distance, allowing him or her to be fast for longer periods of time.

Competition (In-Season)
- Time frame: September–March
- Biomotor abilities trained: reduced volume, strength training, max strength, and flexibility

Preparatory		Competitive		Transition
GPP	SPP	Precomp	Main Comp	Transition

Strength	Accumulation/ max strength	Conversion -power -muscle endurance	Maintenance	Regeneration
Endurance	Aerobic endurance	Foundation of specific endurance	Specific endurance	Aerobic endurance
Speed	Aerobic endurance/ anaerobic endurance	Foundation of speed	Specific speed/agility	

The periodization of main biomotor abilities.[65]

This table depicts the periodization of multiple biomotor abilities during each block (usually four to six weeks) of training. Strength training is slowly converted to strength endurance or power for hockey players. Careful consideration should be taken during this time, as velocities in the weight room fail to replicate those on the ice. Aerobic endurance is slowly converted into sport-specific anaerobic endurance and speed/ acceleration is slowly progressed into application-specific acceleration.

The approach taken in the athlete-centric strength and conditioning program is to slowly move from general to specific in nature. The closer the athlete gets to the upcoming hockey season, the more specific his or her training. Strength, endurance, speed, and lactate capacity are all-important variables trained during this time frame. In contrast, during periods of transition and early preparation, general abilities, such as strength accumulation and aerobic capacity can be trained, as these abilities have less direct transfer to the game of hockey.

- + General fitness (accumulation, aerobic endurance, general speed)
- + Maximal strength

Conversion

- + Strength, endurance, or power
- + Maximal speed

Potential Twelve-Week Periodization Scheme for Various Biomotor Abilities

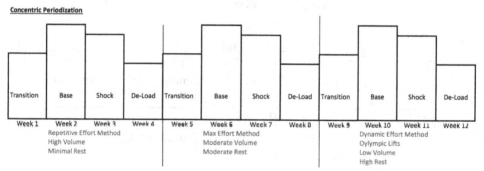

Possible concentric periodization scheme for hockey players based off a twelve-week macrocycle.

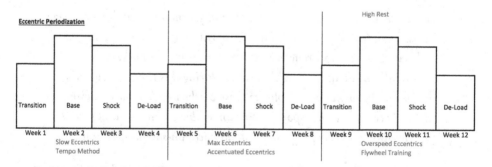

Possible Eccentric periodization scheme for hockey players based off a twelve-week macrocycle.

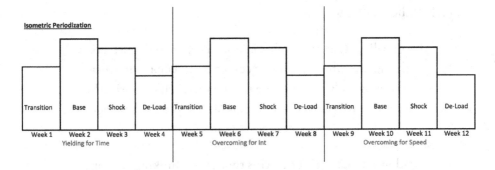

Possible Isometric periodization scheme for hockey players based off a twelve-week macrocycle.

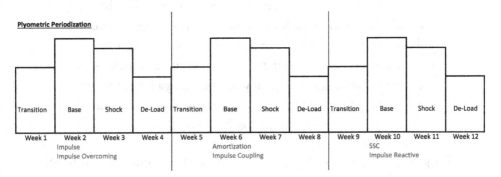

Potential plyometric periodization scheme for hockey players based off a twelve-week macrocycle.

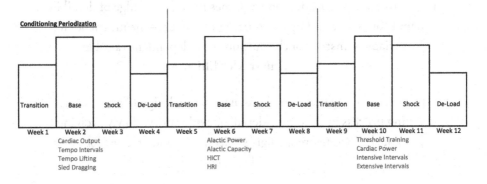

Possible conditioning periodization scheme for hockey players based off a twelve-week macrocycle.

Periodization Models

> I still believe that most collegiate athletes are not much above
> the novice category when it comes to development. They
> need more volume and time to adapt to each exercise. The
> strongest people in the world are well beyond college age.
> —Coach Jeff Connors

> I've read numerous articles on this topic, and thinking that one type
> of periodization scheme is superior than another is like debating
> that a blueberry is better than a strawberry, or vice versa. At the end
> of the day, it depends ... it depends on the athletes, their limiting
> factors, the density and duration of the season, level i.e. youth,
> collegiate, Olympic, professional, goals, etc. Choosing a specific
> periodization scheme thinking it will fit a group of athletes is like
> randomly choosing a floor plan when building a home without
> first asking how many people are going to live in the house.
> —Dr. Brandon Marcello

> The plan must not be so detailed that it affects the manner in which we
> respond to the dynamic nature of daily perturbations in athlete response.
> —Stuart McMillian

> Extensive macro-periodization assumes prior knowledge of detail in
> adaptation; so we end up periodizing the input—the independent
> variable—instead of the output—the dependent variable.
> —Stuart McMillian

> In the absence of ready-made solutions, the design of an efficient
> training process may be considered an exploratory, slowly evolving,
> meticulously documented, single subject, trial and error experiment.
> —John Kiely

It's important to note that models are simply guides, road maps that may
be manipulated each and every day, based on schedule, athlete readiness,
practice schedule, sickness, and injury. The best models are malleable, fluid,
and subject to change on a daily basis. Good programs are sensitive to

low-level threats and also unexpected training opportunities. It is the micro (weekly training) that dictates the macro (monthly/yearly) cycle. Finally, keep in mind that hockey is a team sport and that the competition demands of hockey players are far different from those of the single-sport athlete.

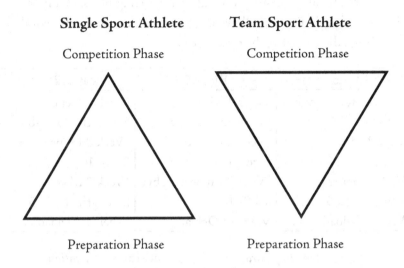

Single Sport Athlete **Team Sport Athlete**

Competition Phase   Competition Phase

Preparation Phase   Preparation Phase

A long, drawn-out competition schedule may have a drastic impact on the preparation phase, leaving the strength coach little time to prepare the athlete for the upcoming season.

Linear periodization incorporates a gradual increase in intensity and a concurrent decrease in total volume. During each successive training block, reps are lowered and weight is increased. Training blocks are typically broken into a hypertrophy phase, a general strength phase, and finally a max strength or power phase. Linear periodization is excellent for beginners but may fall short for advanced lifters. As the initial blocks of training commence, neural qualities may be detrained. As the program advances, metabolic adaptations may be detrained, based on decreased volume.

Hypertrophy	General Strength	Max Strength
Week 1: 2 x 8–10	Week 1: 2 x 5–8	Week 1: 2 x 3–5
Week 2: 3 x 8–10	Week 2: 3 x 5–8	Week 2: 3 x 3–5
Week 3: 3 x 8–10	Week 3: 4 x 5–8	Week 3: 4 x 4–5
Week 4: Deload	Week 4: Deload	Week 4: Deload

Potential loading parameters using linear periodization. Intensity is increased and volume decreased with each successive training block.

Nonlinear or undulating periodization involves drastic alterations between volume and intensity during each training block or microcycle. This form of periodization allows the lifter to focus on both neural and metabolic qualities during the microcycle.

Block 1	Block 2	Block 3
Week 1 Hypertrophy: 2 x 8–10	Week 1 Max Strength: 2 x 3–5	Week 1 General Strength: 2 x 5–8
Week 2 Max Strength: 3 x 3–5	Week 2 General Strength: 3 x 5–8	Week 2 Hypertrophy: 3 x 8–10
Week 3 General Strength: 3 x 5–8	Week 3 Hypertrophy: 4 x 8–10	Week 3 Max Strength: 4 x 3–5
Week 4 Deload	Week 4: Deload	Week 4: Deload

Potential loading parameters using nonlinear periodization where programming variables, such as intensity, volume, tempo, and rest, change with each successive workout.

Concurrent periodization consists of training multiple biomotor qualities during each training block. Power, strength, and speed are all addressed during each respective training session. This is form of periodization may be used for athletes with a lower training age but may be just as relevant for team-sport athletes with short off-seasons.

Monday	Wednesday	Friday
Speed Work: 4x sprints	Speed Work: 4x sprints	Speed Work: 4x sprints
Power Work: 3 x 5	Power: 3 x 5	Power: 3 x 5
General Strength: 3 x 5–8	Max Strength: 3 x 3–5	Hypertrophy: 3 x 8 x 10
Energy System Work	Energy System Work	Energy System Work

Possible weekly loading parameters using the concurrent model. This system allows the lifter to train multiple motor abilities concurrently in one session.

Conjugate periodization allows the athlete to work opposite ends of the absolute strength / absolute speed continuum with concentrated effort. Conjugate periodization was developed by Yuri Verkoshansky and involves training several qualities within one microcycle; however, one quality is heavily developed while the others are maintained. This is a linked system of training. Westside Barbell uses this form of periodization in the planning and training of their power lifters.

Monday	Wednesday	Friday	Sunday
Max Effort Squat/Deadlift 4 x 2, 1 x 1 No more than 10 lifts	Max Effort Bench 4 x 2, 1 x 1 No more than 10 lifts	Dynamic Squat / Deadlift 8–10 x 3 using 50–60% 1RM	Dynamic Bench 8–10 x 3 using 50–60% 1RM

Possible weekly loading parameters using the conjugate model. This system allows the lifter to train both ends of the absolute strength / absolute speed continuum on a weekly basis, as both max force and max velocity are trained within the microcycle.

Block periodization, developed by Vladimir Issurin, is designed for advanced lifters. Sequential blocks of concentrated load are designed, using an accumulation block, transmutation block, and finally a realization block. The unique difference of block periodization is that biomotor abilities are targeted and isolated, while multiple abilities are not trained at once. Issurin states, "The targeted abilities of elite athletes are less accessible to training stimuli than less qualified athletes. Concurrent training for advanced lifters can disrupt physiological adaptation, provoke excessive fatigue, and ultimately decrease the cumulative training effect."[66] Block periodization incorporates high concentrated workloads, a minimal number (usually no more than two) of target abilities within each training block, and consecutive (not concurrent) development of these abilities. Block periodization is based on the belief of training residuals. *Residuals* indicate the length of time various motor abilities can be retained after the cessation of their use. The longer the training residual, the earlier the motor ability can be programmed in the overall plan. The shorter the training residual, the later the motor ability should be programmed to peak the athlete or the sooner it must be reintroduced in order to prevent a detraining effect.

Training Residuals

Motor Ability	Duration
Aerobic endurance	30 +/- 5 days
Max strength	30 +/- 5 days
Glycolytic endurance	18 +/-4 days
Strength endurance	15 +/- 5 days
Max speed	5 +/- 3 days

Issurin's Block Periodization

Accumulation	Transmutation	Realization
Basic strength / submax effort, repeated effort method Rep range: 8–10 Minimal rest	Max strength / max effort method Rep range: 3–5 Increase sets on main lift Increase rest (3–5 min) on main lift	Dynamic effort method/ accommodating resistance Rep range: 1–3 Explosive Rest (3–5 min) on main lift

Potential loading using block periodization. The aim of the process is to slowly move from general to specific. The realization block for hockey players may also be strength endurance. The biggest difference in the process is that only a few motor abilities are trained during each block; others are maintained but not focused on exclusively.

Vertical Integration/High Low

The high-low model was pioneered by world-famous sprint coach Charlie Francis. While training his elite-level sprinters, he found that as training age increased, so did the need for adequate recovery between bouts of high-intensity work. Coach Francis broke running intensities into categories of high and low and called this *vertical integration*. His methodologies eliminated medium-intensity work, or middle ground, as this range was not specific enough for his elite-level athletes and caused too much metabolic disruption, compromising recovery.

High Intensity: 95–100 Percent
- High CNS demand
- Requires complete recovery between exercise and forty-eight hours' rest between next programmed sessions

Medium Intensity: 76–94 Percent
- "Middle ground" avoided
- Takes longer to recover from and causes more metabolic disturbance (This work was also too slow for his sprinters and was eliminated from Charlie's system.)

Low Intensity: 75 Percent or Lower
- Enhances recovery
- Increases parasympathetic tone
- Increases capillary density

Coach Francis states, "By the time training capacity has fully matured, a volume ratio of 35% high and 65% low intensity has proven to be optimal, with high intensity sessions separated by at least 48 hours." (www.CharlieFrancis.com, copyright 2002)

High	Low	High	Low	High	Low	Off
Monday	Tuesday	Wednesday	Thursday	Friday	Saturday	Sunday
High	Low	High	Low	High	Low	Off
Dynamic warm-up	Tempo runs	Dynamic warm-up	Tempo runs	Dynamic warm-up	Tempo runs	
speed	cardiac	speed	cardiac	speed	cardiac	
plyos	output	plyos	output	plyos	output	
strength training	recovery	strength training	recovery	strength training	recovery	
	circuit training		circuit training		circuit training	

From CharlieFrancis.com (2002): The three-times-per-week high-low model programs three days of high-intensity work, separated by three days of low-intensity work and one off day. This model uses training intensities on polar ends of the vertical line shown here, hence, vertical integration.

High	Low	Low	High	Low	Low	Off
Monday	Tuesday	Wednesday	Thursday	Friday	Saturday	Sunday
Dynamic warm-up speed plyos strength training	Tempo runs cardiac output recovery circuit training	Tempo runs cardiac output recovery circuit training	Dynamic warm-up speed plyos strength training	Tempo runs cardiac output recovery circuit training	Tempo runs cardiac output recovery circuit training	

From CharlieFrancis.com (2002), the two-times-per-week high-low model programs two days of high intensity work, separated by three days of low-intensity work, and one off day. This may look more like an in-season program for many athletes. As competition and game schedules pick up, training frequency declines. This model uses training intensities on polar ends of the vertical, hence vertical integration.

During the off-season, the majority of hockey players, including advanced-level competitors, can make excellent gains using nonlinear, concurrent programming. Time, training age, length of competitive season, and training frequency are critical factors when choosing appropriate periodization models. The off-season can range from twelve to sixteen weeks in length. This does not give the strength and conditioning practitioner much time to work with their respective teams. Failure to hit all ends of the neural-metabolic continuum on a weekly basis may leave too little time to sequentially tax these motor abilities (endurance, strength, power, and speed), leaving the player ill-equipped for the demands of the preseason. It is important to note that just because a player plays at an advanced level does not mean that he or she possesses an *advanced* training age. Many elite hockey players are novices in the weight room, and a simple program of escalating intensity can work wonders. Finally, it is important to understand that periodized models were originally designed for individual sports (swimming, weight lifting, and track and field) with a minimal number of events. Hockey is a team sport with a large number of peaks in the form of competition and games. A solid understanding of physiology, time, course of adaptation, and sport schedule will aid the practitioner in choosing the appropriate training model. The model is just a reference. Daily perturbations and fluid manipulation of training variables should be common during the week, as unforeseen events can modify the training schedule, and individual readiness may alter the timing of new training loads. As Mel Siff states,

> Mechanical divisions of training into periods and mesocycles has been based on short-term experience of preparation of athletes during the early stage of formulating the Soviet system of training (1950s) and mainly on the example of three sports, namely swimming, weight lifting and track and field athletics, and therefore cannot be universally applied in its basic form. It is emphasized, that any system of training should be based not so much on logic and empirical experience, but much more on physiology.[67]

Principle 4: Volume

> One cannot have max power with max economy, whether in animals or cars. The key of success is in deciding the highest priority.
> —Thomas Kurz

Volume is the combination of total repetitions performed, frequency, and duration. It can be calculated for each and every exercise or tallied at the conclusion of each workout to calculate the total number of lifts executed and the sessional RPE.

Exercise: 3 x 10 = 30 total repetitions

Workout: 6 total exercises x 12 reps each = 72 TNL (total number of lifts)

Sessional RPE: workout time x RPE (tracks daily load)

Volume is an important variable to consider when designing athletic-based strength programming, as different combinations of sets and repetitions produce drastically altering physiological training effects. Both neural and metabolic adaptations are possible by manipulating repetition schemes, intensity, and overall training volume.

The Repetition Continuum Versus Training Effect[68]

1   3   7   9   11   13   15   17   19   21   23

←--→

100%   50%
Neural Adaptations   Metabolic Adaptations

The repetition continuum shows both neural and metabolic adaptations. Lower rep schemes of increased intensity are programmed to increase max strength and program the CNS to recruit high-threshold motor units. The amount of strength improvement decreases as the number of reps increases. High rep schemes of lower intensity are designed to build general strength, hypertrophy, and strength endurance. High-threshold motor units may still be recruited with high-rep schemes as long as the work performed is to near failure.

Training Implications

Neural/Intensity	Metabolic/Volume
Sets: high 2–10	Sets: low 2–4
Reps: low 1–3	Reps: high 12–15
Load: high 85–100 % 1RM	Load: low <75% 1RM
Rest: high 3–5+ minutes	Rest: low 30–90 seconds

Training variables, such as sets, reps, load, and rest, may be manipulated to train both ends of the neural/metabolic continuum. Volume may be maintained using high-intensity efforts performing more sets, as opposed to adding more reps for low-intensity metabolic efforts.

Volume and intensity are not always inversely related. There are certain periods within program blocks where deliberate pairings of both volume and intensity are increased, decreased, stay the same, or move in different directions. The traditional belief that volume and intensity are inversely related is false. As Pavel Tsatsouline states, "The inverse relationship between volume and intensity is a myth."[69] Each combination serves a result-driven purpose that solicits contrasting adaptations that are appropriate during different stages of the annual plan.

Volume/Intensity Combinations for the Hockey Player

High Volume / Low Intensity—This pairing can be used to build a solid platform of strength endurance by increasing time under tension. This may occur during the conversion phase of the specific preparation block prior to training camp.

Low Volume / High Intensity—This pairing can be used to increase maximal strength via intramuscular tension. This is demanding to the CNS and can be used during the general preparation and competition blocks to avoid delayed soreness during prolonged time under tension.

Medium Volume / Medium Intensity—This is armor building. This pairing can be used for hypertrophy and may be programmed in the early phases of the general preparation period. This is a great pairing for young athletes, as hypertrophy is extremely important during the immediate stages following peak height velocity.

Low Volume / Low Intensity—This is for regeneration. This pairing can be used for recovery / regeneration and is usually programmed as a deload, where volume and intensity are cut 40 to 60 percent. This can be used throughout various portions of the off-season in the general preparation phase, and during the demands of competition to avoid overstressing the player.

High Volume / High Intensity—This is an aggressive pairing that usually leaves athletes on the verge of overreaching or overtraining. Training this way consistently can lead to injury and decreases in performance. This pairing may be used in the final period of the specific preparation period leading up to the demands of preseason.

Volume and intensity are very important program variables; each pairing provides a different stimulus and response. Volume and intensity are not always inversely related. Training age, adaptation being trained, frequency, and competition schedule are critical factors in choosing appropriate training variables.

Off-Season: Creating a Balanced Program for Hockey Players

In his book *A System of Multi-Year Training for Weight Lifters*,[70] A. S. Medveyev proposed two stages of training for weight lifters that are also applicable to hockey players with variable training ages during the off-season. These stages are introduced only after a solid foundation of technical proficiency.

Stage 1
Increase both volume and intensity.
Stage: Beginner/Intermediate
Trainability (the potential to improve): High

Increasing frequency, sets, repetitions, or training intensity on a weekly basis may increase training adaptation for the young athlete. Athletes with minimal training ages can make tremendous gains on a basic program consisting of progressive overload. The goal is to initially increase motor potential and exposure and then slowly increase the capacity to use this newfound motor potential on the ice. The conversion block for max strength incorporates a decrease in volume and an increase in intensity. Conversely, the conversion block for strength endurance will incorporate an increase in volume and a decrease in intensity respectively.

Potential loading methods include the following:
*   *Step loading*—Load is increased progressively from week to week, from training block to training block.

*   *Pyramid loading*—Load and reps are inversely altered (ex: 10 reps at 100lbs / 8 reps at 110lbs / 6 reps at 115 lbs).

*   *Plateau loading*—This loading style is very similar to pyramid loading with a few exceptions: more than one set is performed at each step and there are fewer steps (ex: 10 reps, 10 reps, 8 reps, 8 reps, 6 reps, 6 reps).
*   *Undulated loading*—Wave-like alterations in volume and intensity (ex: week 1, 3 x 10; week 2, 3 x 5; week 3, 3 x 12).

Accumulation Block			General Strength Block			Max Strength Block		
Week	Volume	Intensity	Week	Volume	Intensity	Week	Volume	Intensity
1	3x8	73-75%	1	4x5	78-80%	1	4x3	82-90%
2	4x8	73-75%	2	5x5	78-80%	2	5x3	82-90%
3	4x8	73-75%	3	5x5	78-80%	3	5x3	82-90%
4	2x8	73-75%	4	4x5	78-80%	4	4x3	82-90%
Totals	104 Total Lifts	73-75% 1RM	Totals	90 Total Lifts	78-80% 1RM	Totals	54 Total Lifts	82-90% 1RM

Step loading using linear periodization.

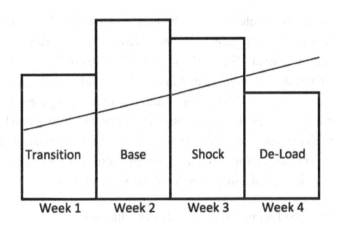

Volume may also be adjusted weekly (as opposed to each block) with different loading parameters.

Transition—Volume is lowered as new intensities and exercises are introduced.

Base loading—The highest volume is experienced during this week of loading.

Shock—Volume is slightly reduced and intensity is increased.

Deload—Intensity is maintained or increased, but volume is dropped.

Stage 2

Stabilize volume and increase intensity.

Stage: Intermediate/Advanced

Trainability: Low

One important thing to understand is that the more experienced a trainee is, the less he will benefit from the rep and set schemes on the right side of each graph (metabolic adaptations) and the bigger the effect of methods on the left side will be. This is why as you gain experience you should increase your average training intensity, decrease the number of reps per set, and increase the number of sets per exercise.

—Christian Thibaudeau

Increasing total volume can only work so long for advanced trainees; volume is recovery dependent. When recovery is compromised, so are potential training gains. Strength and conditioning coach Ian King states, "I question the elevation of volume in the absence of concurrent ability to maintain intensity."[71] Athletes with advanced training ages need to focus on maintaining volume while increasing intensity. The conversion block for max strength incorporates a decrease in volume and an increase in intensity. Conversely, the conversion block for strength endurance will incorporate an increase in volume and a decrease in intensity respectively.

Potential loading methods include the following:
+ *Wave loading*—Wave loading alters neuromuscular inhibition to allow the system to produce a greater degree of force as measured by load lifted. Loads should be strategically programmed to enhance the loading potential of the second wave (ex. 3 at 100lbs / 2 at 110lbs / 1 at 120lbs— first wave; 3 at 105lbs / 2 at 115lbs / 1 at 125lbs—second wave).
+ *Concentrated loading*—Concentrated loading is marked by an increase of both volume and intensity during the loading phase. This form of loading is not sustainable for long periods of time as such intense stimulus placed on the athlete may compromise recovery, regeneration, and long-term gains.
+ *Cluster loading*—Cluster loading is programmed during blocks of maximal strength. Cluster loading consists of a series of one rep max efforts with minimal rest (fifteen to thirty seconds) in between. This rest gives the lifter a break between highly demanding CNS work and provides the coach with an opportunity to assess technique and further refine movement inefficiencies that would otherwise not be addressed during the lift.

♦ *Contrast loading*— 6/1, 6/1, 6/1. Perform 3 groups each with a: 90-2 min rest in between. Use approximately 80% 1RM for reps of 6, and 95% for reps of 1.

Accumulation Block			General Strength Block			Max Strength Block		
Week	Volume	Intensity	Week	Volume	Intensity	Week	Volume	Intensity
1	3x8	76-78%	1	5X4	78-80%	1	4x3	76-91%
2	4x8	76-78%	2	6X3, 1X4	76-89%	2	1X3,2,1, 1X3, 2,1	80-94%
3	4x8	76-78%	3	6X3, 1X4	76-89%	3	1X3,2,1, 1X3, 2,1	89-94%
4	2x8	76-78%	4	5X4	75-86%	4	1X3,2,1, 1X3, 2,1	89-94%
Totals	104 Total Lifts	76-78% 1RM	Totals	84 Total Lifts	75-89% 1RM	Totals	48 Total Lifts	76-94% 1RM

Please note that although percentages are used as examples, the body responds to perceived effort and stress differently each day. No organism responds in linear fashion, and each individual responds differently to stress. Consequently the coach is urged to individually monitor load with minimal use of percentage-based charts.

> There are no 'absolute phenomena' in biology. Everything is time- and space-bound. The animal or plant or micro-organism ... is but a link in an evolutionary chain of changing forms, none of which has any permanent validity
> —Max Delbruck

The body does not recognize percentages when training intensity is prescribed. It recognizes effort and perceived exertion. These variables may change daily. Use the former only as a guide when programming.
—Brett Bartholomew

Assessing the Year-Round Volume for Hockey Players

Sport schedule dictates programming variables. Seasonal fluctuations in sporting demands prompt reciprocal fluctuations in volume and intensity.
—Anthony Donskov

> *Stress experienced on the ice* = < *stress in the weight room*
> < *Stress experienced on the ice* = > *stress in the weight room*

In-season stress and recovery—The goal is to manage this relationship and create balance so that players may perform on the ice during competitive periods. Physical preparation, training frequency, and overall training volume are reduced.

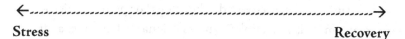

Stress   **Recovery**

➢ Hockey   Sleep
➢ Competition Calendar   Nutrition
➢ Outside stressors   Hydration
➢ Physical Preparation   Meditation/Breathing

Off-season stress and recovery—The goal is to manage this relationship and create balance; however, the major source of stress has now changed. Physical preparation, training frequency, and overall volume are increased.

Stress   **Recovery**

➢ Physical Preparation   Sleep
➢ Outside Stressors   Nutrition
                                  Hydration
                                  Meditation/Breathing

Balancing the stress-recovery relationship for hockey players requires scrutinizing the demands of schedule. Ebbs and flows in the training process should mimic those found in the annual calendar. Each training block builds on one another, creating a solid foundation of performance enhancement while minimizing performance decrements.

Year Round Volume: General Guidelines

General Preparation (May-June)	Specific Preparation (July-August)	Competition (September-May)	Transition (April)
Volume: High **Rep Ranges:** 6-10 **Intensity:** 70-82+% 1RM **Rest:** Low **Adaptation:** General Strength/Capacity.	**Early Period** **Volume:** Low **Rep Ranges:** 3-5 **Intensity:** 75%-90+% 1RM **Rest:** High **Adaptation:** Max Strength, Power. **Late Period** **Conversion:** Strength Endurance **Volume:** High **Rep Ranges:** 8-10 **Intensity:** 66%-80% 1RM **Rest:** Low **Adaptation:** Strength Endurance.	**Volume:** Low **Rep Ranges:** 3-5 **Intensity:** 60%-90% 1RM **Rest:** High **Adaptation:** Max Strength, Power, recovery.	**Volume:** Moderate **Rep Ranges:** 10-12 **Intensity:** 62-75% 1RM **Rest:** Low **Adaptation:** General Strength/Capacity.

The hockey schedule dictates programming variables. Off-season gains can be made from building foundational strength and converting this motor ability into strength endurance. The competition schedule is a time to reduce training volume.

Final Thoughts

- For young, growing hockey players, volume using submaximal weight is important. As training age increases, volume maintains its importance in the presence of increased intensity.
- Intensity is slowly increased during the general and specific preparation periods, building up to the competition phase.
- Most hockey players should train between the five and eight rep ranges for strength qualities.
- Five reps is a great scheme for easy strength. World-renowned power lifter Ed Coan states, "The five-rep set strikes the best balance between low one-to-three rep power-building sets and eight-to-twelve tissue-building sets."
- Athletes with minimal training ages (less than two and a half years in the weight room) should focus on movement first and then the addition of volume and general strength over time. This can be accomplished with a basic progressive resistance program.
- For minimal training age, adjust volume and intensity every four to six weeks.
- For advanced training age, adjust volume and intensity frequently.

Potential Four-Week Loading Block for an Advanced Hockey Player

Week 1	Transition block	Introduction to new training methods 3 x 5 at 85% max
Week 2	Base loading	Volume maximal during this week 1 x 5 at 85% max, 3 x 4 at 85–90%
Week 3	Shock loading	Intensity maximal during this week 4/3/2/4/3/2 (87%/90%/95%) (90%/95%/98%)
Week 4	Deload	Volume cut abruptly during this week, approximately 50% 2 x 5

- Athletes with higher training ages (three to five or more years) should seek to maintain volume and increase intensity. Constant fluctuations in variables such as intensity and volume enable the coach to develop a sustainable program while avoiding overtraining and stagnation.

- "A quick study of most of the successful strength-sport coaches will reveal a common theme: very few exercises, relatively consistent loading from cycle to cycle, and a focus on technical mastery" (Stuart McMillian).

- Each end of the neural-metabolic continuum can be used during conversion phases prior to the hockey season. High load, low volume (the left side of the continuum) will solicit max strength and power and CNS stimulation, while high volume, low load (right side of the continuum) will solicit strength endurance gains via metabolic disturbance.

Conversion Block

Neural or Power   Metabolic or Capacity

←--→

Max Strength	Strength Endurance
High Load	Low Load
Low Volume	High Volume

- High-volume workouts can cause substantial physiological damage. For this reason, volume should be reduced during the in-season.
- High-intensity, low-volume work is great during the demands of the competitive season, as it minimizes metabolic accumulation and prevents soreness.
- "Absolute/max strength is the glass; everything else (speed, conditioning, power, etc.) is just the liquid. The bigger the glass, the more liquid it can hold" (Dan John).
- Never push past technical proficiency.
- When in doubt, less is more.
- Training is *not* a sport. Hockey is played on the ice, not in the weight room. Always assess risk versus reward.

Principle 5: Athlete Readiness and Effective Dose

> For every substance, small doses stimulate, moderate doses inhibit, and large doses kill. —L. Garkavi

A difficult task for the strength and conditioning professional is to gauge appropriate dose response in prescribing effective stress and adequate restoration. Tools, such as Omegawave, HRV (ANS), and vertical jump (CNS), offer objective feedback, while subjective stress scores offer subjective feedback. The practitioner may use all measures to assess athlete readiness and current trainability levels. The goal is for athletes to train as hard as they are *ready* to train. Strength Coach Ian King refers to this as capable versus optimal and states, "You may be capable, but is it optimal? Don't focus on how hard you can train, rather focus on how hard you should train."[72] The athlete-centric program is athlete-driven, as training variables fluctuate regularly, depending on the readiness of the athlete. This allows the program to be malleable, flexible, and fluid by nature. Readiness is assessed daily, as this affects programming variables, such as volume, intensity, and external load.

> **Readiness**—current functional state of the athlete
> **Internal Load**—the athlete's reaction/response to external load
> **External Load**—weight on the bar

Poor Readiness = >Internal Load < External Load
Increase in Readiness = < Internal Load > External Load
Athletes with high readiness can sustain higher external loads while minimizing residual fatigue, exhaustion, and high internal load markers.

Stress

The body reacts to stress (mechanical, physiological, and psychological) in the same universal manner with the release of stress hormones that provide a fight-or-flight response. Chronic activation of this response, regardless of modality, may lead to overtraining, illness, or injury. With regards to strength training and conditioning, coaches may experience two types of overtraining with their athletes: Basedowic and Addisonic.

Basedowic overtraining resembles Basedow's disease (enlarged thyroid) in which the sympathetic nervous system is overreactive during rest (excitation of CNS). This can cause the resting heart rate to rise and may be the result of too much high-intensity training (i.e., too much lactate, a decrease in pH). Treatment includes rest and a special diet (foods high in alkali to neutralize pH).

Addisonic overtraining resembles Addison's disease (inability of adrenals to release hormones) where the system stays in a parasympathetic state (inhibition of CNS). This may result from high-volume, excessive work leading to exhaustion. Athletes often state, "I step on the gas and nothing happens."[73] Treatment involves avoiding high-volume protocol.

"An optimal 'system in balance' occurs when sympathetic system is active during work and parasympathetic is active during rest. Overtraining is the result of an imbalance of stimulation and inhibition of the CNS."[74]

Sympathetic	Parasympathetic
Fight or flight	Rest and digest
Increased heart rate	Decreased heart rate
Increased blood pressure	Decreased blood pressure
Low blood pH	Neutral blood pH
Tension	Relaxation
High-intensity exercise	Low-intensity exercise

Subjective Stress and the Brain

Subjective ratings of mood, fatigue, stress, and soreness may be our most cost effective prevention strategy (regarding overtraining).
—Kreider, Fry, and O'Toole *Overtraining in Sport*

The use of subjective information, taken prior to and at the conclusion of the workout, may aid the strength coach in providing a user-friendly feedback tool, indicating the athlete's current state of readiness. Subjective feedback arrives to the brain via the sensory system. This system is responsible for collecting information about the internal and external environment and communicating this information to higher centers in the brain. Subjective feedback is more or less how the athlete feels and is his or her current emotional state.

Subject Stress Scores Measure Training Effects

▫ Immediate Effect—the stress of a single bout of exercise (catabolic)
▫ Residual Training Effect—the regeneration process after exercise (anabolic)
▫ Cumulative Training Effect—the attempt to capitalize on the advantage in which regeneration outpaces stress (immediate + residual effects)

The goal of a well-run strength and conditioning program is to increase the trainability, or the functional state, of the athlete. Subjective stress scores seek to measure immediate, residual, and cumulative training effects, giving the practitioner better information when prescribing individual load.

Subjective information is easy to attain and economically efficient to monitor, as opposed to blood testing and saliva swabs, which take time, cost money, and are inconvenient to administer for most working professionals. In addition new hypotheses of fatigue are emerging around the central idea that the brain (a.k.a. "central governor") is the master regulator in responding to fatigue and cumulative stress. A governor simply prevents a system from going all out. As exercise physiologist Professor Tim Noakes explains, "We now believe that fatigue is purely an emotion affected by factors, such as motivation and drive, memory of prior activity, and other emotions, such as anger or fear." Although this model has been used to explain fatigue in ultraendurance sports, such as marathon running, its ideologies may be considered when designing athletic-based programs and assessing cumulative bouts of stress placed on the athlete. Noakes continues, "This model predicts that max exercise capacity is a process coordinated subconsciously by the brain. When oxygenation approaches the limits of what is safe, the brain's motor cortex, which recruits the exercising muscles, is informed, and it stops recruiting additional muscle."[75] Could this also be the case for increased perceived internal load in the weight room? The master regulator of the neuroendocrine system is the hypothalamus. This area of the brain is responsible for triggering hormonal responses to anything that may alter homeostasis, including weight training and various forms of conditioning. "It is likely that neuroendocrine changes accompanying overtraining are very much related to alterations in immune function."[76] The hypothalamus communicates directly with the pituitary gland to form the HPA (hypothalamic pituitary axis) and is responsible for growth hormone production, thyroid stimulation and calorigenesis, fight-or-flight response, and the synthesis of androgens.

The Master Regulator

The hypothalamus can fail under the demands of heavy training
(Barron et al. 1985). Prolonged heavy training, associated with
repetitive large stress hormone response (e.g. Catecholamines,
ACTH, cortisol, prolactin), will cause the body to respond by down
regulating specific hormone receptors in the target tissues, making
these tissues less responsive to the effects of these hormones.
—*Immune Function*

Cellular aspects of overtraining: increase creatine kinase activity, elevated
cortisol levels, decrease muscle glycogen and testosterone, alteration
of shape of mitochondria with decreased mitochondrial enzymes.
—Kreider, Fry, and O'Toole, *Overtraining in Sport*

The master control system of the autonomic nervous system is of utmost importance in understanding stress, neuroendocrine function, and how overtraining may affect performance. The hypothalamus and pituitary release several hormones in response to stress. The body always seeks homeostasis. Repetitive bouts of stress without adequate rest and recovery may alter the system, down-regulate hormone release, and blunt receptor affinity. The goal for the athlete is to recover more efficiently from the stimulus being prescribed by the coach. The hypothalamic pituitary axis is responsible for the following hormones released at various times in the stress-recovery process:

Hypothalamic-Pituitary-Growth Hormone (HPGH) Axis
+ Growth hormone is an important metabolic hormone that stimulates net protein anabolism, lipolysis, and linear bone growth. Growth hormone is released during REM sleep.

Hypothalamic-Pituitary-Thyroid (HPT) Axis

+   These hormones modulate calorigenesis and protein, carbohydrate, and lipid metabolism.

Hypothalamic-Pituitary-Adrenal (HPA) Axis

+   The HPA, together with the autonomic nervous system, is the most important system of the body. This modulates the fight-or-flight response and is heavily affected by chronic stress and overtraining. The inability of this system to shut down many times is due to high-volume, high-intensity workloads with inadequate rest and regeneration.

Hypothalamic-Pituitary-Gonadal (HPG) Axis

+   The gonads are stimulated to synthesize and secrete androgens, estrogens, and progestins by the concerted action of luteinizing hormone. The hypothalamus plays a part in this process by secreting gonadotropin-releasing hormone.

Changes in the hypothalamus disrupt homeostasis and create an unfavorable neuroendocrine environment. Subjective stress scores seek to maintain balance in autonomic functioning and prevent long, drawn-out periods of overreaching. These scores empower the strength coach to assess trends in loading and to accurately administer appropriate dosage relative to the athlete's current state of readiness.

Administering Subjective Stress Scores

Subjective ratings are taken twice during each training period, prior to the workout and at the conclusion of the workout.

Preworkout Stress = athlete's current readiness.
RPE = response to external load.

Preworkout Stress

Prior to the workout commencing, the athlete will choose a number from one to five, based on their current stress levels. The four best predictors of overtraining are: fatigue, muscle soreness, stress, and quality of sleep.[77] This numbering system ranks these variables into one single stress score. The testing scores are broken down as follows:

- 1 = feeling fresh 100 percent
- 2 = fresh/motivated
- 3 = slightly motivated/tired
- 4 = tired / sore / feeling stressed
- 5 = exhausted /sick / stressed / sore

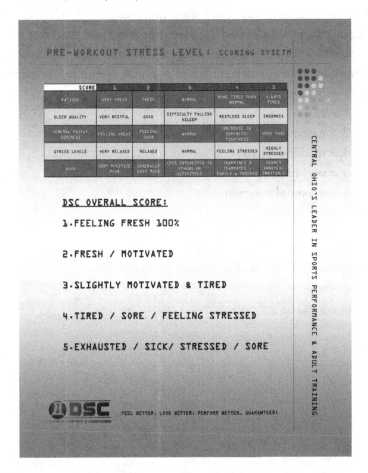

Athletes are asked to assess their current readiness levels based on overall fatigue, sleep quality, general muscle soreness, current stress levels, and mood. Once these variables have been graded one to five, all columns are calculated and divided by five to give the practitioner an overall mean preworkout stress number. This score can be used to monitor stress levels over time, assess trends in response to stimulus, and modify variables, such as volume and intensity, to fit the individual needs of the athlete.

Ratings of Perceived Exertion

At the conclusion of the workout, athletes will again score one to five based on the difficulty level of the workout. This is called the ratings of perceived exertion (RPE). RPE can also be used after each set to assess the difficulty level experienced by the athlete. As strength coach Brett Bartholomew states, "The body does not recognize percentages when training intensity is prescribed. It recognizes effort and perceived exertion. These variables may change daily. Use the former only as a guide when programming." Immediate feedback in response to load can be established by simply using a rating system.

- 1 = easy
- 2 = moderate
- 3 = moderate/hard
- 4 = very hard
- 5 = maximal exertion

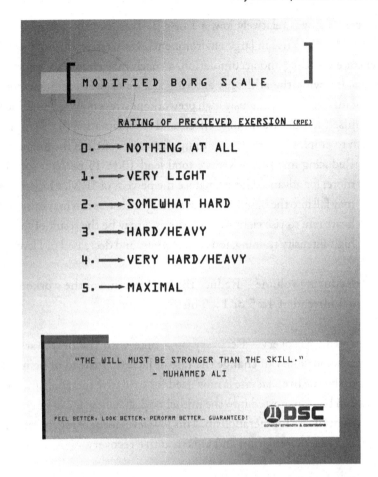

[MODIFIED BORG SCALE]

RATING OF PRECIEVED EXERSION (RPE)

0. ——▶NOTHING AT ALL

1. ——▶VERY LIGHT

2. ——▶SOMEWHAT HARD

3. ——▶HARD/HEAVY

4. ——▶VERY HARD/HEAVY

5. ——▶MAXIMAL

"THE WILL MUST BE STRONGER THAN THE SKILL."
- MUHAMMED ALI

FEEL BETTER, LOOK BETTER, PEROFRM BETTER... GUARANTEED! DSC

Swedish physiologist Gunnar Borg originally designed the RPE scale with fifteen categories, ranging from six (very easy) to twenty (extremely hard). This scale has been modified for ease and simplicity in the weight room for various populations of intermediate and advanced lifters. Use RPE after each rep to adjust external load and at the conclusion of the workout to grade overall difficulty of the training session.

The System

The system is designed to assess trends over periods of time (microcycles/mesocycles) and direct snapshots of stress and perceived efforts, which may change daily. If an athlete attends a training session with high levels of preworkout stress, a four or a five stress level, the coach may have the athlete refer to his or her program and identify a previous workout when his or her respective RPE was relatively low, a 1 or a 2. This form of deload is athlete specific and easy to use in large environments. Conversely, during periods of concentrated loading and accumulation, a coach may choose to ignore these numbers, knowing the athlete is entering a state of overreaching prior to a deload or off week. Continuously high preworkout stress numbers may indicate compromised cumulative training effects and maladaptation that may prompt the coach to employ other programming alterations such as the following:

- Reducing intensity—Reduce total load 10 to 15 percent, sometimes more; for advanced lifters, reduce the percent of 1RM. Hockey players may fall into the Basedowic overtraining bucket, as this may cause resting heart rate to rise eight to ten beats and may be the result of too much high-intensity training, too much lactate, and decreased pH levels.

- Reducing volume—Reduce the total volume of the workout (ex. 2 x 5 instead of 4 x 5 or 1 x 5 instead of 3 x 5).

- Active Recovery—Recovery on a bike with the heart rate in the aerobic zone can change the fate of lactate. Instead of being taken up by the liver, lactate is now used for oxidative metabolism. Lactate can be transported into the mitochondria, where it can be converted to pyruvate for metabolism. This low-level form of regeneration also increases circulation and aids in active recovery.

- Planned Rest—Rest has a dramatic effect on the acid-base status of the muscle. Active rest clears metabolic by-products formed during glycolysis, and static rest restores phosphocreatine stores. In addition, deload weeks may be planned for the last week of the mesocycle and recovery days may be added to give athletes additional time away from the gym to restore, recover, and refresh.

- Pharmaceutical Interventions—Supplementation can aid in expediting the regeneration process, such as a postworkout recovery protein drink, fish oil, creatine, sports drinks, and amino acids. In addition, adequate sleep (eight to ten hours), hydration, and diet are critical components in the regeneration process. Lack of these essential recovery tools can drive the stress response into sympathetic mode and alter the function of the hypothalamus.

- Therapeutic intervention—Tissue quality (foam roll, static stretch, dynamic warm-up), warm baths, floating, and light massage can shift the system into a more parasympathetic state, promoting a decrease in tissue density and an increase in systemic circulation.

Many times, a picture doesn't tell the whole story. A duck looks cool and calm above the water but underneath may be exhausted trying to stay afloat. These forms of regeneration as just described attempt to see the real picture and are easy to administer. In the end, the job of the strength and conditioning practitioner is to be as accurate as possible in the prescription of stress. Many times, more is not better. In fact, from the experience of the author, less is best—one Tylenol or fifteen? Which doctor would you visit?

Subjective readings seek to understand what the coach may not see, what lies underneath the waters. Accumulated stress comes in many forms, much of which may be above and beyond that experienced during mechanical loading in the weight room.

Subjective stress scores are far from perfect. An environment built on trust, accountability, and accurate record keeping provides coaches an opportunity to individualize an appropriate balance between stress and recovery, making sure an athlete is ready to train at the highest load, while simultaneously avoiding an accumulation of fatigue across multiple training weeks.

DSC ADP Winter '17 - Phase 1										

Pre-Workout Stress:

1-Feeling Great 100%, 2-Motivated + feeling sore, 3- Slightly motivated + Tired, 4-Tired + Sore, 5- Exhausted+Sick.

Day 1	Tempo	Rest	WK1	Grade +/-/+	Reps	WK 2	Grade +/-/+	Reps	WK 3	Grade +/-/+	Reps
A1.) VBT: Concentric Squat Jump		:90			x5			x5			x5
Speed: 1.2m/s-1.3 m/s		:90			x5			x5			x5
								x5			x5
A2.) Spiderman					2x3			2x3			2x3
B1.) Eccentric Double KB FS	(3/0/0)	:90			x6-8			x5-7			x5-7
	(3/0/0)	:90			x6-8			x5-7			x5-7
								x5-7			x5-7
B2.) SA Face Pull w/reach					x6-8			x5-7			x5-7
					x6-8			x5-7			x5-7
								x5-7			x5-7
B3.) TGU (to elbow)					3x3			3x3			3x3
C1.) Partner Assisted Nordic Cur	(3/0/0)	:90			x6-8			x5-7			x5-7
	(3/0/0)	:90			x6-8			x5-7			x5-7
								x5-7			x5-7
C2.) Half Kneeling BU KB OH Press					x6-8			x6-8			x6-8
					x6-8			x6-8			x6-8
								x6-8			x6-8
C3.) Farmer's Walk					x3			x3			x3
RPE (Rating of Percieved Exertion)											

Preworkout stress levels are documented prior to the assigned workload. This gives coaches the ability to gauge appropriate dose responses during individual training sessions and to assess trends during mesocycles. Response to external loads may also be documented after each working set by simply grading the weight one to five or using the +/-/= system to track resistance gains. Finally, RPE may be used to gauge the difficulty of the overall workload.

Review

The five principles of athletic-based programming aid the practitioner in designing appropriate strength and conditioning programs for both youth- and elite-level hockey players. These principles are the pillars of program design and serve as foundational bedrock for both means and methods. There is a plethora of methods that can be used to elicit various physiological adaptations; however, it is the few guiding principles in which methods are applied that make or break an athletic-based program.

1) *Train Movement Patterns*—Hockey players are not bodybuilders, power lifters, Olympic lifters, CrossFit competitors, or strongmen. Pattern-specific work ensures the nervous system is working as

one functional unit, improves movement variability, increases total range of motion and impulse, and enhances performance. Pushing and pulling patterns (vertical and horizontal), knee- and hip-dominant patterns may be prioritized by volume or sequence in order to build athlete-specific symmetry, while avoiding chronic overuse patterns associated with sport.

2) *Big Rocks*—The system and the sum of its parts is more powerful than the same system being isolated into separate components. Compound, multijoint movements under load serve as foundational lifts for hockey players. In the weight room, these lifts can simultaneously improve isolation-based exercise; however, many times, it does not work in opposition. Isolation-based lifts are not specific to the demands of sport or function of the nervous system. If these lifts are to be used, they should be scheduled early in the off-season during general preparation work. Think of injecting a performance-enhancing drug. It does not work on one area of the body; the entire system is stimulated. This holds true for weight training. Bigger, stronger, and more powerful arms and shoulders are produced by lifting heavy things from the floor, taxing the entire system, not performing arm curls and triceps extensions. Big rocks are lifts that provide positive transfer to sport. The more transfer, the better the athlete may use this newfound capacity to enhance on-ice skill and physical performance.

3) *Periodization*—Periodization is accomplished by breaking the training cycle into manageable periods for the hockey player. Periodization creates ebbs and flows in the training process and is underpinned with the ideology that peak performance is not an everyday occurrence. The goal of strength training is to allow the athlete to express his or her strength at the right time. In the 1960s, Matveyev was the first practitioner to suggest that the year be divided into three categories: preparation (adaptation), competition (application), and transition (regeneration). The length of each period is determined by the competition calendar. Each period is characterized with varying manipulations of load, intensity, work-to-rest, and physiological targets. Periodization creates process and purpose in the training plan and provides structure for both athlete

and coach. Periodization does not have a bias toward a particular training theory but simply assists in planning, structuring, and managing athletic-based performance. Although annual planning is popular among the coaching profession, it is important not to look too far ahead in the process. Future adaptations are best understood in the present tense. The micro should dictate the macro; as weekly readiness may be subject to change, so should the coaches' decision-making abilities and programming variables. The longer the period of time for the plan, the less applicable the plan will be. Programming needs to be sensitive to emerging information.

Youth athletes with minimal training ages can sustain increases in both volume and intensity, as their nervous systems develop postpeak height velocity. A basic linear program with progressive resistance is excellent for development. Once the athlete has advanced in weight-room experience maintenance or a decrease in volume is experienced in order for the magnitude of the stimulus to increase. Intensity is greatest during this time. Nonlinear, conjugate, block, or high/low programming is now a more sustainable model for the advanced athlete.

4) *Volume*—Different combinations of volume and intensity create altering physiological training adaptations. Volume and intensity are programming variables that can be manipulated frequently— at the conclusion of each mesocycle and at the conclusion of each microcycle. Fluctuations are based on sporting schedule, competition calendar, training age, and programming goals. As sprint Coach Stuart McMillian states, "Great coaches have consistent loading among cycles, as the more consistent the stimulus, the better prediction of future stimuli we can predict."

Programming Means Dictated by Volume and Intensity

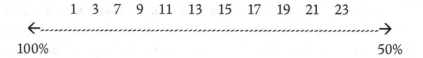

1   3   7   9   11   13   15   17   19   21   23

←---→

100%   50%

Low Volume / High Intensity	***High Volume / Low Intensity***
Acyclic work	Cyclic work
Neural adaptations	Metabolic adaptations
Olympic lifting	Hypertrophy
Med ball work	Strength endurance
Max effort method	Circuit training
Dynamic effort method	Repetitive effort method
Jump training	

Programming using low volume / high intensity is neural in nature and sits to the far left of the continuum. These exercises typically occur during the onset of weight training, as the nervous system is fresh. In contrast, metabolic adaptations sitting to the far right of the continuum are created using high-volume and low-intensity protocol. This causes more physiological damage to the tissue, as time under tension is increased and the acid base of the muscle is dramatically altered in the form of reduced pH.

For the beginner/intermediate-aged lifter, increasing both volume and intensity is important. During the formative years in sport training, hypertrophy work and volume reign supreme. Strength Coach Dan John refers to this as the inverse S curve of hypertrophy.

Inverse S Curve of Hypertrophy, courtesy of Dan John

Beginner/Intermediate Lifter—This is typically the first four to six years of a structured strength-training program. The athlete's chronological age during this period of development ranges from approximately thirteen to eighteen years of age. This is a critical window in the development of the athlete, as most young, inexperienced trainees lack under-the-bar experience, motor control, and base levels of strength. As Strength Coach Charlie Francis states, "Beginners cannot generate enough output to overload their nervous system, even though all their training is at the high end of their current capacity." Progressive resistance, armor building, hypertrophy, increased volume, and time under tension are all important training considerations in this early developmental stage. This time period represents the initial upward slope of the inverse S.

Intermediate/Advanced—This period occurs after the athlete has had significant time in the weight room, mastered basic technique, and exhausted any gains made by using basic standard progressive resistance protocol. The athlete's chronological age during this period of refinement ranges from twenty to thirty years old, during the peak of one's athletic career. Volume is increased until gains are neutralized. At this point, volume is dropped. Sprint Coach Charlie Francis states,

> The overall volume of training increases sharply during the early years, but eventually it becomes impossible for the athlete to tolerate increase in both intensity and volume. As intensification is the prime objective, volume must stabilize to allow intensity to predominate. Eventually, high-level performers must drop the volume of training to continue the intensification required for the most advanced stages of their careers. (www.CharlieFrancis.com, copyright 2002)

During this time, biomotor abilities, such as max strength and power; highly demanding CNS work; and specific speed training are addressed. Restoration is of prime importance during this time, as complete recovery between reps and sessions provides intended adaptation and regeneration. Full recovery between reps ensures that the nervous system is fresh and ready for increased demands, and recovery between sessions is maximized by at least forty-eight hours before a repeat stimulus is being administered. Athletes should attempt to recover with the same intensity as they train. This period represents the major downslope of the inverse S curve.

Postretirement—After one's hockey career is over and elite athletic performance is no longer needed for sport, one experiences a shift in training targets. Age is accompanied with a loss in bone-mineral density, coupled with a decrease in lean muscle mass (sarcopenia), altered hormone secretion (decreased testosterone, increased cortisol), and increased external stressors from family, job, additional commitments, and so on. During this period, hypertrophy work once again becomes important. This period represents the second upward slope of the inverse S curve.

5) *Readiness*—Stress causes an initial decrease in function, followed by an adaptation (recovery) that improves function. An imbalance between stress and recovery can cause stagnation and maladaptation. The goal is to provide overload, a blend of volume and intensity that stimulates the nervous system without causing long-term overtraining and performance decrements. There is enormous variability in each athlete's ability to respond to training demands. Everyone is different, and the same workout may yield completely altering responses based on body type, injury history, outside stressors, and lifestyle.

Overtraining causes cellular imbalances that compromise homeostasis in the body—changes, such as "increased creatine kinase activity, elevated cortisol levels, decreased muscle glycogen and testosterone, alteration of shape of mitochondria with decreased mitochondrial enzymes."[78] Testing athletes can be both expensive and time-consuming. Using subjective scores to measure stress and manipulate programming variables offers a cheap alternative and may be one of the greatest prevention strategies. Rating mood, fatigue, stress, and soreness can aid the practitioner in prescribing a more appropriate dose response. Readiness is measured using the following:

- Preworkout stress scores—This is based on mood, fatigue, stress, and soreness. How do you feel prior to the workout? 1 (100%) to 5 (exhausted/sick/stressed).
- Postworkout RPE—How hard was the training session? 1 (nothing at all) and 5 (maximal).
- In-session RPE—An important reminder when programming is that the body does not recognize training percentages, it recognizes perceived effort and sensation. How did the weight feel? 1 (easy) to 5 (maximal). This is a simple way to manipulate intensity during each set.

- Load Score—Session-RPE involves multiplying training intensity using an RPE scale by training duration in minutes to create a training impulse score normally referred to as *load*.[79]

Daily Training Workloads

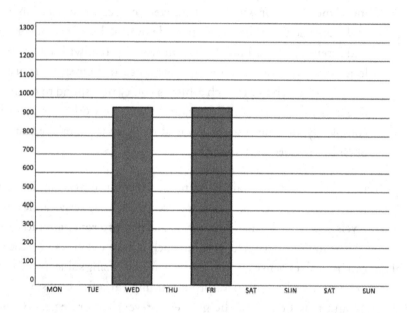

Sessional RPE used to measure daily workloads.

In addition, other steps can be taken by the practitioner to enhance recovery means and heighten adaptation.

- The addition of rest days (minimum of one week)—The more demand on the CNS, the more rest is needed for recovery. It is better to undertrain than to overtrain.
- The implementation of low-intensity days—Charlie Francis was fond of saying, "Trash the CNS anywhere, it will show up everywhere." Low-intensity days are meant for recovery and regeneration.
- Fluctuate volume and intensity to match the competition calendar. For example, during the in-season, hockey games are the major stressor experienced by the player. Training during this time serves an auxiliary means. However, during the off-season, hockey games are no longer played and strength training means are now shifted

as the prime stressors. This is accompanied by an increase in both volume and intensity respectively.

▫ Flush rides in the aerobic zone reduce the acidity of the muscles following glycolytic work through oxidation of end-product metabolites.

▫ Static rest is needed to fully recover phosphocreatine stores after short, intense work.

▫ Therapy sessions, such as massage, foam rolling, and saunas are all methods used to enhance recovery. Just as in strength training, there is considerable variability in how each and every athlete responds to therapy. Therapy, such as deep-tissue massage, is a form of stress. Different regeneration methods are used at different periods in the training cycle.

Sympathetic Dominant	Parasympathetic Dominant
Active Recovery Training	**Active Recovery Training**
Relaxation/regeneration, soft-tissue therapy	Intensive deep-tissue massage
Hot-water therapy	Cold-water immersion
Deep-water floating/swimming	Contrast therapy
Mental relaxation techniques	Sauna
Acupuncture	Change of environment

Slide courtesy of Joel Jamieson.[80] Advanced recovery and regeneration strategies. There is considerable variability in how each athlete responds to therapy and recovery strategies. If these interventions have never been used, they should not be considered close to competition because of the uncertainty of bodily response. Both sympathetic and parasympathetic tone can be measured using heart rate variability and measuring resting heart rate on a daily basis. Large increases in resting heart rate (eight to ten beats per minute) shift the body into a sympathetic state. In contrast, low resting heart rate levels with minimal energy may shift the body into a parasympathetic state. Active recovery training attempts to reverse these trends, restoring balance and homeostasis.

Chapter 8

Sample Off-Season Weight Training Programs

Programming Essentials:
+ Needs analysis
+ Movement assessment
+ Performance assessment
+ Goals
+ Program
+ Monitor
+ Retest

By the time the practitioner is ready to write the program, four of the seven bullets of the program checklist should be completed.

Program Checklist

Information	Check List
1. Needs Analysis	✓
2. Movement Assessment	✓
3. Performance Assessment	✓
4. Goals	✓
5. Program	Write the Program
6. Monitor	Monitor Results
7. Retest	Re-test movement and performance

Programming Pre Requisites

1	• Physiological Reasoning
2	• Philosophy
3	• Periodization
4	• Planning
5	• Program Design

This graph has been modified from the work of Mladen Jovanovic.

To truly master the art of programming, the practitioner needs to understand basic physiology, in particular the time course for adaptation for various qualities. This should be meshed with a strong philosophy. Physiological reasoning and philosophy are the most important when designing programs. Periodization and planning are of secondary importance.

Program 1: Beginner/Intermediate Program

Two times a week, nonlinear, concurrent programming—speed and power work are done prior to the onset of weight training.

The following is a two-week sample program that can be used for beginner/intermediate hockey players in the off-season during the general preparation period. The program is concurrent, which means that multiple motor abilities are trained each day. Speed and power work are done prior to weights, as these are more demanding on the CNS. When multiple biomotor abilities need to be improved in minimal time, which is the case in most off-season circumstances, concurrent programming is an excellent model to implement.

Accumulation/Hypertrophy Block (Mid-May to Mid-June: Four-Week Block)

Mon/Wed	Tue/Thurs/Fri
□ Basic strength / hypertrophy, submax effort □ Rep range: 6–8 □ Intensity: 70–80% 1RM □ Minimal rest	□ Cardiac output □ Tempo method

⬛DSC
DONSKOV STRENGTH & CONDITIONING

Name:

DSC ADP Summer '16 - Phase 1

Pre-Workout Stress:

1-Feeling Great 100%, 2-Motivated + feeling sore, 3- Slightly motivated + Tired, 4-Tired + Sore, 5- Exhausted+Sick.

Day 1	Tempo	Rest	WK1	Grade +/-/+=	Reps	WK 2	Grade +/-/+=	Reps	WK 3	Grade +/-/+=	Reps
A1.) KB Jump		:90			x5			x5			x5
		:90			x5			x5			x5
								x5			x5
A2.) Plank					2 x :30			2 x :35			2 x :40
B1.) Double KB FS	(3/0/0)	:90			x6-8			x6-8			x6-8
OR Goblet Squat	(3/0/0)	:90			x6-8			x6-8			x6-8
								x6-8			x6-8
B2.) Neutral Grip Chin Up	(3/0/0)				x6-8			x6-8			x6-8
OR SA Lat Pull Down	(3/0/0)				x6-8			x6-8			AMRAP
								x6-8			x6-8
B3.) Kneeling Pallof (flexion/extension)					2x5			2x5			2x5
C1.) Partner Assisted Nordic Curl	(3/0/0)	:90			x6-8			x6-8			x6-8
OR VG Leg Curl	(3/0/0)	:90			x6-8			x6-8			x6-8
								x6-8			x6-8
C2.) Half Kneeling BU KB OH Press					x6-8			x6-8			x6-8
					x6-8			x6-8			x6-8
								x6-8			x6-8
C3.) Farmer's Walk					x3			x3			x3
RPE (Rating of Percieved Exertion)											

Pre-Workout Stress:											
1-Feeling Great 100%, 2-Motivated + feeling sore, 3- Slightly motivated + Tired, 4-Tired + Sore, 5- Exhausted+Sick.											

Day 2	Tempo	Rest	WK1	Grade +/-/+=	Reps	WK 2	Grade +/-/+=	Reps	WK 3	Grade +/-/+=	Reps
A1.) KB Jump		:90			x5			x5			x5
		:90			x5			x5			x5
								x5			x5
A2.) Side Plank					2x:35			2x:40			2x:45
B1.) Eccentric DB Bench Press	3/0/0	:90			x6-8			x6-8			x6-8
	3/0/0	:90			x6-8			x6-8			x6-8
	3/0/0							x6-8			x6-8
B2.) Trap Bar DL					x6-8			x6-8			x6-8
					x6-8			x6-8			x6-8
								x6-8			x6-8
B3.) Kneeling Anti-Rotation w/rope					2x5			2x5			2x5
C1.) KB Bat Wing		:90			x:20			x:25			x:30
		:90			x:20			x:25			x:30
								x:25			x:30
C2.) Split Squat					x6-8			x6-8			x6-8
					x6-8			x6-8			x6-8
								x6-8			x6-8
C3.) Farmers Walk					x3			x3			x3
RPE (Rating of Percieved Exertion)											

The goal of this phase is to build a solid foundation of general strength and aerobic capacity. The exercises selected have a lower transfer of training. In addition, two-week programs are full body in nature, taxing all patterns each day (pushing, pulling, knee dominant, and hip dominant) with an emphasis on prioritizing two major patterns. The other two major patterns are emphasized on day 2. The last week of the block is used as a deload.

Max Strength Block (Mid-June to Mid-July: Four Weeks)

Mon/Wed	Tue/Thurs/Fri
□ Max strength / max effort method	□ Cardiac power
□ Rep range: 5–7	□ Threshold training
□ Intensity: 80–90% 1RM	□ Alactic power
□ Increase sets on main lift	□ Alactic capacity
□ Increase rest (3–5 min.) on main lift	

Anthony Donskov

Name:

DSC ADP Summer'16 - Phase 2

Pre-Workout Stress:
1-Feeling Great 100%, 2-Motivated + feeling sore, 3- Slightly motivated + Tired, 4-Tired + Sore, 5- Exhausted+Sick.

Day 1	Tempo	Rest	WK1	Grade +/-/+=	Reps	WK 2	Grade +/-/+=	Reps	WK 3	Grade +/-/+=	Reps
A1.) Squat Jump		2:00			x5			x5			x5
		2:00			x5			x5			x5
								x5			x5
A2.) Suite Case Carry					3 x 3			3 x 3			3 x 3
B1.) Front Squat	(2/2/0)	2:00			x5-7			x5-7			x5-7
	(2/2/0)	2:00			x5-7			x5-7			x5-7
					x5-7			x5-7			x5-7
B2.) Cannonball Chin Up					x5-7			x5-7			x5-7
					x5-7			x5-7			x5-7
								x5-7			x5-7
C1.) RDL	(2/2/0)	2:00			x5-7			x5-7			x5-7
	(2/2/0)	2:00			x5-7			x5-7			x5-7
								x5-7			x5-7
C2.) Half Kneeling Alt. OH Press					x5-7			x5-7			x5-7
					x5-7			x5-7			x5-7
								x5-7			x5-7
C3.) Half Kneeling Pallof (flexion/extension)					2x5			2x5			2x5
RPE (Rating of Percieved Exertion)											

Pre-Workout Stress:
1-Feeling Great 100%, 2-Motivated + feeling sore, 3- Slightly motivated + Tired, 4-Tired + Sore, 5- Exhausted+Sick.

Day 2	Tempo	Rest	WK1	Grade +/-/+=	Reps	WK 2	Grade +/-/+=	Reps	WK 3	Grade +/-/+=	Reps
A1.) Squat Jump		2:00			x5			x5			x5
		2:00			x5			x5			x5
								x5			x5
A3.) Spiderman					2x3			2x3			2x3
B1.) BB Bench Press	(2/2/0)	2:00			x5-7			x5-7			x5-7
	(2/2/0)	2:00			x5-7			x5-7			x5-7
					x5-7			x5-7			x5-7
								x5-7			x5-7
B2.) Trap Bar DL					x5-7			x5-7			x5-7
					x5-7			x5-7			x5-7
								x5-7			x5-7
C1.) Half Kneeling Cable Row	(2/2/0)	2:00			x5-7			x5-7			x5-7
	(2/2/0)	2:00			x5-7			x5-7			x5-7
								x5-7			x5-7
C2.) RFESS					x5-7			x5-7			x5-7
					x5-7			x5-7			x5-7
								x5-7			x5-7
C3.) Half Kneeling Anti-Rotation					2x5			2x5			2x5
RPE (Rating of Percieved Exertion)											

The goal of this phase is to increase max strength by increasing the sets of the main lift and spreading the volume accordingly. An increase in rest is programmed, coupled with a pairing of restorative work (mobs, dynamic stretches, and so on). All patterns are taxed (pushing, pulling, knee dominant, and hip dominant) with an emphasis on prioritizing two major patterns. The other two major patterns are emphasized on day 2. The last week of the block is used as a deload.

Strength Endurance Block (Mid-July to August: Four to Six Weeks)

188

Mon/Wed	Tue/Thurs/Fri
□ Repeat effort method / AMRAPs □ Rep range: 10+ □ Intensity: 60–73% 1RM □ Strength endurance □ Rest: minimal	□ Lactate power intervals □ Lactate capacity intervals

DSC

Name:

DSC ADP Summer '16 - Phase 3

Pre-Workout Stress:

Day 1	Tempo	Rest	WK1	Reps	WK2	Reps
Double KB FS				x10		x10
				x10		x10
				x10		x10
KB Cross Carry				x1		x1
				x1		x1
HK Alt OH Press				x10		x10
				x10		x10
				x10		x10
Split Squat				x10		x10
				x10		x10
				x10		x10
Plank Reach				x5		x5
				x5		x5
				x5		x5
TRX Row				x20		x20
				x20		x20
				x20		x20
BW Squat				x10		x10
				x10		x10
				x10		x10
Shoulder Scaption				x10		x10
				x10		x10
				x10		x10
KB Row				x10		x10
				x10		x10
				x10		x10
Kneeling Pallof Flex/Ext				x10		x10
				x10		x10
				x10		x10
RPE (Rating of Percieved Exertion)						

Pre-Workout Stress:							
Day 2	Tempo	Rest	WK1	Reps	WK2	Reps
50's Bench Press				amrap		amrap
choose weight to attain 50				amrap		amrap
reps in 3 sets—~65% of 1RM				amrap		amrap
Partner MB Chest Pass				x5		x5
				x5		x5
				x5		x5
KB Circuit						
SLDL				x8		x8
				x8		x8
				x8		x8
Chin Ups				x8		x8
				x8		x8
				x8		x8
Plank Pulls				x8		x8
				x8		x8
				x8		x8
Push Ups				x8		x8
				x8		x8
				x8		x8
Reverse Lunge				x10		x10
				x10		x10
				x10		x10
HK Face Pull				x1		x1
				x1		x1
				x1		x1
RPE (Rating of Percieved Exertion)						

The goal of this phase is to transfer max strength into strength endurance and ready the hockey player for the demands of training camp. Load is reduced, and rest is minimized, placing great demands on endurance and the ability to contract in the presence of lactate accumulation. All patterns are taxed (pushing, pulling, knee dominant, and hip dominant) with an emphasis on prioritizing two major patterns. The other two major patterns are emphasized on day 2. The last week of the block is used as a deload.

Program 2: Four Times a Week, Nonlinear, Concurrent Programming

Speed and power work are done prior to the onset of weight training.

The four-times-a-week sample program can also be used for beginner and intermediate hockey players in the off-season during the general preparation period. The biggest difference between the frequency of a two-times-a-week program and a four-times-a-week program is the movement sequencing. The two-per-week program focuses on two full-body lifts during the course of the training week. In contrast, the four-a-week program divides the patterns further.

Monday	Tuesday	Thursday	Friday
Knee dominant	Horizontal push	Hip dominant	Horizontal pull
Vertical pull	Horizontal pull	Vertical push	Horizontal push
Core	Core	Core	Core

or

Monday	Tuesday	Thursday	Friday
Knee dominant	Horizontal push	Hip dominant	Horizontal pull
Hip dominant	Horizontal pull	Knee dominant	Horizontal push
Vertical pull	Core	Vertical push	Core

Anthony Donskov

Block 1: ACCUMULATION											

NAME: _____

Pre-Workout Stress:

1-Feeling Great 100%, 2-Motivated + feeling sore, 3- Slightly motivated + Tired, 4-Tired + Sore, 5- Exhausted+Sick.

Day 1	Tempo	Rest	WK1	M/S	Reps	WK 2	M/S	Reps	WK 3	M/S	Reps
A1.) KB Swing		2:00			x5			x5			x5
		2:00			x5			x5			x5
								x5			x5
A2.) Spiderman					2x3			2x3			2x3
B1.) Double KB Front Squat	(3/0/0)	:90			x6-8			x6-8			x6-8
	(3/0/0)	:90			x6-8			x6-8			x6-8
	(3/0/0)	:90			x6-8			x6-8			x6-8
								x6-8			x6-8
B2.) Yeilding Chin Up					x:35			x:40			x:40
					x:35			x:40			x:40
								x:40			x:40
C1.) Partner Assisted Nordic Curl	(3/0/0)	:90			x6-8			x6-8			x6-8
	(3/0/0)	:90			x6-8			x6-8			x6-8
								x6-8			x6-8
C2.) Half Kneeling BU KB Press					x6-8			x6-8			x6-8
					x6-8			x6-8			x6-8
								x6-8			x6-8
C3.) Farmers Walk					x3			x3			x3
RPE (Rating of Percieved Exertion)											

192

Pre-Workout Stress:											
Day 2	Tempo	Rest	WK1	M/S	Reps	WK 2	M/S	Reps	WK 3	M/S	Reps
A1.) DB Bench Press	3/0/0	:90			x6-8			x6-8			x6-8
	3/0/0	:90			x6-8			x6-8			x6-8
	3/0/0	:90			x6-8			x6-8			x6-8
	3/0/0							x6-8			x6-8
A2.) Posterior shoulder mob w/band					x5 breaths			x5 breaths			x5 breaths
					x5 breaths			x5 breaths			x5 breaths
								x5 breaths			x5 breaths
B1.) KB Bat Wings		:90			x:20			x:25			x:30
		:90			x:20			x:25			x:30
								x:25			x:30
B2.) Push Ups	3/0/0				x6-8			x6-8			x6-8
	3/0/0				x6-8			x6-8			x6-8
								x6-8			x6-8
B3.) TRX Row	3/0/0				x6-8			x6-8			x6-8
	3/0/0				x6-8			x6-8			x6-8
								x6-8			x6-8
B4.) Tall Kneeling Lift					3x8			3x8			3x8
RPE (Rating of Percieved Exertion)											

Anthony Donskov

Pre-Workout Stress:											

1-Feeling Great 100%, 2-Motivated + feeling sore, 3- Slightly motivated + Tired, 4-Tired + Sore, 5- Exhausted+Sick.

Day 3	Tempo	Rest	WK1	M/S	Reps	WK 2	M/S	Reps	WK 3	M/S	Reps
A1.) KB Swing		2:00			x5			x5			x5
		2:00			x5			x5			x5
								x5			x5
A2.) Ankle Rocks					2 x 5			2 x 5			2 x 5
B1.) Trap Bar		:90			x6-8			x6-8			x6-8
		:90			x6-8			x6-8			x6-8
		:90			x6-8			x6-8			x6-8
								xAMRAP			xAMRAP
B2.) Half Kneeling Face Pull					x6-8			x6-8			x6-8
					x6-8			x6-8			x6-8
								x6-8			x6-8
C1.) Spit Squat		:90			x6-8			xG-8			x6-8
		:90			x6-8			x6-8			x6-8
								x6-8			x6-8
C2.)Shoulder Scaption					x6-8			x6-8			x6-8
					x6-8			x6-8			x6-8
								x6-8			x6-8
C3.) Famers Walk					x3			x3			x3
RPE (Rating of Percieved Exertion)											

194

Pre-Workout Stress:											
Day 4	Tempo	Rest	WK1	M/S	Reps	WK 2	M/S	Reps	WK 3	M/S	Reps
A1.) Incline DB Bench Press		:90			x6-8			x6-8			x6-8
		:90			x6-8			x6-8			x6-8
		:90			x6-8			x6-8			x6-8
								xAMRAP			xAMRAP
A2.) Kneeling band W's					x8			x8			x8
					x8			x8			x8
								x8			x8
B1.) BB Row		:90			x6-8			x6-8			x6-8
		:90			x6-8			x6-8			x6-8
								x6-8			x6-8
B2.) Push Ups					x6-8			x6-8			x6-8
					x6-8			x6-8			x6-8
								x6-8			x6-8
B3.) Half Kneeling Cable Row					x6-8			x6-8			x6-8
					x6-8			x6-8			x6-8
								x6-8			x6-8
B4.) Tall Kneeling Chop					3x8			3x8			3x8
RPE (Rating of Percieved Exertion)											

General Strength

195

BLOCK 2: STRENGTH

NAME: _____

| Pre-Workout Stress: | | | | | | | | | | |

1-Feeling Great 100%, 2-Motivated + feeling sore, 3- Slightly motivated + Tired, 4-Tired + Sore, 5- Exhausted+Sick.

Day 1	Tempo	Rest	WK1	M/S	Reps	WK 2	M/S	Reps	WK 3	M/S	Reps
A1.) VBT Hang Clean (Power Pos.)		2:00			x5			x5			x5
1.2-1.3 m/s		2:00			x5			x5			x5
								x5			x5
A2.) Spiderman w/reach					2x3			2x3			2x3
B1.) VBT Camberd Bar Front Squat	(2/1/0)	2:00			x4-6			x4-6			x4-6
<.50 m/s	(2/1/0)	2:00			x4-6			x4-6			x4-6
	(2/1/0)	2:00			x4-6			x4-6			x4-6
								x4-6			xAMRAP
B2.) Cannonball Grip Chin Up					x4-6			x4-6			x4-6
					x4-6			x4-6			xAMRAP
								x4-6			x4-6
C1.) Beam Bar RDL	(2/1/0)	2:00			x4-6			x4-6			x4-6
	(2/1/0)	2:00			x4-6			x4-6			x4-6
								x4-6			x4-6
C2.) HK Landmine OH Press					x4-6			x4-6			x4-6
					x4-6			x4-6			x4-6
								x4-6			x4-6
C3.) Suite Case Carry					x3			x3			x3
RPE (Rating of Percieved Exertion)											

Pre-Workout Stress:											
Day 2	Tempo	Rest	WK1	M/S	Reps	WK 2	M/S	Reps	WK 3	M/S	Reps
A1.) VBT Fat Bar Bench Press	(2/1/0)	2:00			x4-6			x4-6			x4-6
<.50 m/s	(2/1/0)	2:00			x4-6			x4-6			x4-6
	(2/1/0)	2:00			x4-6			x4-6			x4-6
	(2/1/0)							x4-6			xAMRAP
A2.) Kneeling Wall Shoulder Handcuffs					x10			x10			x10
					x10			x10			x10
								x10			x10
B1.) KB Row		2:00			x4-6			x4-6			x4-6
		2:00			x4-6			x4-6			x4-6
								x4-6			x4-6
B2.) Half Kneeling Cable Press	(2/1/0)				x4-6			x4-6			x4-6
	(2/1/0)				x4-6			x4-6			x4-6
								x4-6			x4-6
B3.) 1 Arm TRX Row w/offset KB	(2/1/0)				x4-6			x4-6			x4-6
	(2/1/0)				x4-6			x4-6			x4-6
								x4-6			x4-6
B4.) Half Kneeling Lift					3x8			3x8			3x8
RPE (Rating of Percieved Exertion)											

| Pre-Workout Stress: | | | | | | | | | | | |

1-Feeling Great 100%, 2-Motivated + feeling sore, 3- Slightly motivated + Tired, 4-Tired + Sore, 5- Exhausted+Sick.

Day 3	Tempo	Rest	WK1	M/S	Reps	WK 2	M/S	Reps	WK 3	M/S	Reps
A1.) VBT Hang Clean (Power Pos.)		2:00			x5			x5			x5
1.2-1.3 m/s		2:00			x5			x5			x5
								x5			x5
A2.) Diagonal Hip Mob					2 x 3			2 x 3			2 x 3
B1.) VBT Speed Sumo DL		2:00			x4-6			x4-6			x4-6
.90-1.0 m/s		2:00			x4-6			x4-6			x4-6
		2:00			x4-6			x4-6			x4-6
								x4-6			x4-6
B2.) ISO Face Pull					x4-6			x4-6			x4-6
					x4-6			x4-6			x4-6
								x4-6			x4-6
C1.) RFESS		2:00			x4-6			x4-6			x4-6
		2:00			x4-6			x4-6			x4-6
								x4-6			x4-6
C2.) Shoulder Circuit					x4-6			x4-6			x4-6
					x4-6			x4-6			x4-6
								x4-6			x4-6
C3.) Suite Case Carry					x3			x3			x3
RPE (Rating of Percieved Exertion)											

Pre-Workout Stress:											
Day 4	Tempo	Rest	WK1	M/S	Reps	WK 2	M/S	Reps	WK 3	M/S	Reps
A1.) VBT Speed Incline Bench Press		2:00			x4-6			x4-6			x4-6
.90-1.0 m/s		2:00			x4-6			x4-6			x4-6
		2:00			x4-6			x4-6			x4-6
								x4-6			x4-6
A2.) Standing band W's					x10			x10			x10
					x10			x10			x10
								x10			x10
B1.) DB Row		2:00			x4-6			x4-6			x4-6
		2:00			x4-6			x4-6			x4-6
								x4-6			x4-6
B2.) FE Push Ups	(0/3/0)				x4-6			x4-6			x4-6
	(0/3/0)				x4-6			x4-6			x4-6
								x4-6			x4-6
B3.) ISO Cable Row					x4-6			x4-6			x4-6
					x4-6			x4-6			x4-6
								x4-6			x4-6
B4.) Half Kneeling Chop					3x8			3x8			3x8
RPE (Rating of Percieved Exertion)											

Max Strength

Block 3: Max Strength/Power

NAME: _____

Pre-Workout Stress:

1-Feeling Great 100%, 2-Motivated + feeling sore, 3- Slightly motivated + Tired, 4-Tired + Sore, 5- Exhausted+Sick.

Day 1	Tempo	Rest	WK1	M/S	Reps	WK 2	M/S	Reps	WK 3	M/S	Reps	WK 4	M/S	Reps
A1.) Hang Clean (Mid Thigh.): VBT		2:00			x3			x3			x3			x3
1.2-1.3 M/S		2:00			x3			x3			x3			x3
								x3			x3			x3
A2.) Goblet Squat to Press					2x8			2x8			2x8			2x8
B1.) SL Squat	(1/0/0)	3:00			x4-6			x3-5			x3-5			x6-8
	(1/0/0)	3:00			x4-6			x3-5			x3-5			x6-8
	(1/0/0)	3:00			x4-6			x3-5			x3-5			x6-8
								x3-5			x3-5			x6-8
B2.) Trap Bar Press					x4-6			x3-5			x3-5			x6-8
					x4-6			x3-5			x3-5			x6=8
								x3-5			x3-5			x6-8
C1.) BB SLDL	(1/0/0)	3:00			x4-6			x3-5			x3-5			x6-8
	(1/0/0)	3:00			x4-6			x3-5			x3-5			x6-8
								x3-5			x3-5			x6-8
C2.) Candlestick Grip Chin Up					x4-6			x3-5			x3-5			x6-8
					x4-6			x3-5			x3-5			x6-8
								x3-5			x3-5			x6-8
C3.) Prone KB Shift					3x5			3x5			3x5			3x5
RPE (Rating of Percieved Exertion)														

200

Pre-Workout Stress:														
Day 2	Tempo	Rest	WK1	M/S	Reps	WK 2	M/S	Reps	WK 3	M/S	Reps	WK 4	M/S	Reps
A1.) Chain Bench Press: VBT	1/0/0	3:00			x4-6			x3-5			1x1x1			x6-8
	1/0/0	3:00			x4-6			x3-5			1x1x1			x6-8
	1/0/0	3:00			x4-6			x3-5			1x1x1			x6-8
	1/0/0							x3-5			1x1x1			x6-8
A2.) TRX Y's					x4-6			x3-5			x8			x8
					x4-6			x3-5			x8			x8
								x3-5			x8			x8
B1.) KB Fat Grip Row					x4-6			x3-5			x3-5			x6-8
					x4-6			x3-5			x3-5			x6-8
								x3-5			x3-5			x6-8
B2.) Split Stance Cable Press	1/0/0				x3-5			x3-5			x3-5			x6-8
	1/0/0				x3-5			x3-5			x3-5			x6-8
								x3-5			x3-5			x6-8
B3.) 1 Arm Cable Rotational Ro	1/0/0				x4-6			x3-5			x3-5			x6-8
	1/0/0				x4-6			x3-5			x3-5			x6-8
								x3-5			x3-5			x6-8
B4.) Standing Lift					3x8			3x8			3x8			3x8
RPE (Rating of Percieved Exertion)														

Pre-Workout Stress:													

1-Feeling Great 100%, 2-Motivated + feeling sore, 3- Slightly motivated + Tired, 4-Tired + Sore, 5- Exhausted+Sick.

Day 3	Tempo	Rest	WK1	M/S	Reps	WK 2	M/S	Reps	WK 3	M/S	Reps	WK 4	M/S	Reps
A1.) Hang Clean (Mid Thigh): VBT		2:00			x3			x3			x2			1x1x1
1.2-1.3 M/S		2:00			x3			x3			x2			1x1x1
								x3			x2			1x1x1
A2.) Wall HF Mob					2 x 8			2 x 8			2 x 8			2 x 8
B1.) Kbox Squat		3:00			x4-6			x3-5			x3-5			x6-8
		3:00			x4-6			x3-5			x3-5			x6-8
		3:00			x4-6			x3-5			x3-5			x6-8
								x3-5			x3-5			x6-8
B2.) SA Face Pull w/reach					x4-6			x3-5			x3-5			x6-8
					x4-6			x3-5			x3-5			x6-8
								x3-5			x3-5			x6-8
C1.) Kbox RDL		3:00			x4-6			x3-5			x3-5			x6-8
		3:00			x4-6			x3-5			x3-5			x6-8
								x3-5			x3-5			x6-8
C2.) Shoulder Box					x4-6			x3-5			x3-5			x6-8
					x4-6			x3-5			x3-5			x6-8
								x3-5			x3-5			x6-8
C3.) TGU (to bridge)					x3			x3			x3			x3
RPE (Rating of Percieved Exertion)														

Pre-Workout Stress:														
Day 4	Tempo	Rest	WK1	M/S	Reps	WK 2	M/S	Reps	WK 3	M/S	Reps	WK 4	M/S	Reps
A1.) Speed Incline Bench Press: VBT		3:00			x3-5			x3-5			x3-5			x6-8
1.2-1.3 M?S		3:00			x3-5			x3-5			x3-5			x6-8
		3:00			x3-5			x3-5			x3-5			x6-8
								x3-5			x3-5			x6-8
A2.) Band ER					x8			x8			x8			x8
					x8			x8			x8			x8
								x8			x8			x8
B1.) Neutral Grip Bar Row					x4-6			x3-5			x3-5			x6-8
					x4-6			x3-5			x3-5			x6-8
								x3-5			x3-5			x6-8
B2.) SA DB Press w/TB					x4-6			x3-5			x3-5			x6-8
					x4-6			x3-5			x3-5			x6-8
								x3-5			x3-5			x6-8
B3.) Standing SA/SL Cable Row					x3-5			x3-5			x3-5			x6-8
					x3-5			x3-5			x3-5			x6-8
								x3-5			x3-5			x6-8
B4.) Standing Chop					3x8			3x8			3x8			3x8
RPE (Rating of Percieved Exertion)														

Specific Preparation

Anthony Donskov

Block 4: Conversion

NAME: _____

Pre-Workout Stress:

1-Feeling Great 100%, 2-Motivated + feeling sore, 3- Slightly motivated + Tired, 4-Tired + Sore, 5- Exhausted+Sick.

Day 1	Tempo	Rest	WK1	M/S	Reps	WK 2	M/S	Reps	WK 3	M/S	Reps
A1.) VBT: Hang Clean		2:00			x1x1x1			1x1x1			1x1x1
1.2-1.3m/s		2:00			1x1x1			1x1x1			1x1x1
								1x1x1			1x1x1
A2.) Hurdle Jumps					2x5			2x5			2x5
B1.) RFESS	(1/0/0)	3:00			x6-8			x6-8			x6-8
	(1/0/0)	3:00			x4-6			x4-6			x4-6
Pair w/3x6 Continuous Lateral	(1/0/0)	3:00			x3-5			x3-5			x3-5
Hurdle Hops								x3-5			x3-5
B2.) Candlestick Chin Up					x6-8			x6-8			x6-8
					x4-6			x4-6			x4-6
Pair w/3x5 Continuous MB Slam								x3-5			x3-5
C1.) BB Reverse Lunge	(1/0/0)				x6-8			x6-8			x6-8
	(1/0/0)				x4-6			x4-6			x4-6
								x3-5			x3-5
C2.) Trap Bar Press					x6-8			x6-8			x6-8
					x4-6			x4-6			x4-6
								x3-5			x3-5
C3.) KB Revrerse Crunch					3x12			3x12			3x12
RPE (Rating of Percieved Exertion)											

Pre-Workout Stress:												
Day 2	Tempo	Rest	WK1	M/S	Reps	WK 2	M/S	Reps	WK 3	M/S	Reps
A1.) VBT: Cluster Bench Press	1/0/0	3:00			1x1x1			x5			x5
.25-.65m/s	1/0/0	3:00			1x1x1			1x1x1			1x1x1
	1/0/0	3:00			1x1x1			1x1x1			1x1x1
	1/0/0							1x1x1			1x1x1
A2.) MB Chest Pass					x5			x5			x5
					x5			x5			x5
								x5			x5
B1.) Fat Grip BB Row		3:00			x6-8			x6-8			x6-8
		3:00			x4-6			x4-6			x4-6
								x3-5			x3-5
B2.) Explosive Push Ups	0/0/0				x6-8			x6-8			x6-8
	0/0/0				x4-6			x4-6			x4-6
								x3-5			x3-5
B3.) Supine MB Chest Throw	0/0/0				x6-8			x6-8			x6-8
	0/0/0				x4-6			x4-6			x4-6
								x3-5			x3-5
B4.) Standing Chop					3x8			3x8			3x8
RPE (Rating of Percieved Exertion)											

Pre-Workout Stress:										
1-Feeling Great 100%, 2-Motivated + feeling sore, 3- Slightly motivated + Tired, 4-Tired + Sore, 5- Exhausted+Sick.										
Day 3	Tempo	Rest	WK1	M/S	Reps	WK 2	M/S	Reps	WK 3	M/S	Reps
A1.) VBT: Hang Clean		2:00			x3			x3			x3
1.2-1.3m/s		2:00			x3			x3			x3
								x3			x3
A2.) Adductor Mob					2 x 3			2 x 3			2 x 3
B1.) VBT: Trap Bar Jump		3:00			x6-8			x6-8			x6-8
1.0-1.3 m/s		3:00			x4-6			x4-6			x4-6
Pair w 3x5 Lateral Bound		3:00			x3-5			x3-5			x3-5
								x3-5			x3-5
B2.) Half Kneeling Face Pull					x6-8			x6-8			x6-8
					x4-6			x4-6			x4-6
								x3-5			x3-5
C1.) Skater Squat		3:00			x6-8			x6-8			x6-8
		3:00			x4-6			x4-6			x4-6
Pair w/ 3x5 Continuous Hurdle Jumps								x3-5			x3-5
C2.) TRX Y's					x6-8			x6-8			x6-8
					x4-6			x4-6			x4-6
								x3-5			x3-5
C3.) Famers Walk					**x3**			**x3**			**x3**
RPE (Rating of Percieved Exertion)											

Pre-Workout Stress:											
Day 4	Tempo	Rest	WK1	M/S	Reps	WK 2	M/S	Reps	WK 3	M/S	Reps
A1.) VBT: Narrow Grip Bench Press		3:00			x6-8			x6-8			x6-8
1.0-1.3m/s		3:00			x4-6			x4-6			x4-6
		3:00			x3-5			x3-5			x3-5
								x3-5			x3-5
A2.) MB Throw/Explode					x2			x2			x2
					x2			x2			x2
								x2			x2
B1.) Cable Rotational Row		3:00			x6-8			x6-8			x6-8
		3:00			x4-6			x4-6			x4-6
								x3-5			x3-5
B2.) SA Incline Press w/tennis	0/0/0				x6-8			x6-8			x6-8
	0/0/0				x4-6			x4-6			x4-6
3x5 Approaching MB Side trow								x3-5			x3-5
B3.) SA/SL Cable Row	0/0/0				x6-8			x6-8			x6-8
	0/0/0				x4-6			x4-6			x4-6
								x3-5			x3-5
B4.) Standing Lift (use plates)					3x8			3x8			3x8
RPE (Rating of Percieved Exertion)											

Conversion

Program 3 (Advanced): Four Times per Week, Nonlinear, Conjugate Programming

This form of periodization is for hockey players with advanced training experience. Both ends of the absolute strength, absolute speed continuum are trained during the week with concentrated effort on one of these qualities. Reps are kept low, ensuring maximal intensity during max effort days and bar velocity during dynamic effort days. This is a linked system of training. Westside Barbell uses this form of periodization in the planning and training of their power lifters. It can be modified and used to train hockey players with advanced training experience in the weight room. Special consideration should be given when choosing foundational and auxiliary lifts, as the demands of hockey are far different from those faced by a power lifter. Intensity should be monitored at all times. Allowing the athlete to consistently leave a few reps in the bank ensures safety and potential injury.

Monday	Wednesday	Friday	Sunday
Max effort squat / deadlift 4 x 2, 1 x 1 no more than 10 lifts	Max effort bench 4 x 2, 1 x 1 no more than 10 lifts	Dynamic squat / deadlift 8–10 x 3 using 50–60% 1RM	Dynamic bench 8–10 x 3 using 50–60% 1RM

Possible weekly loading parameters using the conjugate model.
Repetition schemes are chosen using the Prilepin table.

Prilepin Table Set/Rep Schemes

	Percent	Reps per set	Optimal	Range
Speed Strength	55-65	4-6	24	18-30
Strength End	70-75	4-6	18	12-24
Strength/Hyper	80-85	2-4	15	10-20
Max Strength	Above 90	1-2	7	4-10

Set/Rep Schemes: Prilepin Table 55-65%   Target Adaptation: Speed Strength

Reps	1	2	3	4	5	6
Set Schemes				x6	x6	x5
				x5	x5	x4
					x4	x3

Set/Rep Schemes: Prilepin Table 70-75%   Target Adaptation: Strength Endurance

Reps	1	2	3	4	5	6
Set Schemes				x6	x4	x4
				x4	x3	x3
				x3		x2

Set/Rep Schemes: Prilepin Table 80-85%   Target Adaptation: Strength/Hypertrophy

Reps	1	2	3	4	5	6
Set Schemes		x10	x6	x5		
		x9	x5	x4		
		x8	x4	x3		
		x7				
		x6				
		x5				

Set/Rep Schemes: Prilepin Table 90% +   Target Adaptation: Max Strength

Reps	1	2	3	4	5	6
Set Schemes	x10	x5				
	x9	x4				
	x8	x3				
	x7	x2				
	x6					
	x5					
	x4					

Possible set/rep schemes for hockey players using the Prilepin Table

Phase 1
Pre-Workout Stress:

Day 1	Tempo	Rest	Week 1	Reps	Week 2	Reps	Week 3	Reps
TB Loaded Jump	Exp	2:00		x5		x5		x5
				x5		x5		x5
				x5		x5		x5
KB SL Sit Up				2x8		2x10		2x12
Sumo DL	(1/0/0)	3:00		x2		x2		x2
	(1/0/0)	3:00		x2		x2		x2
	(1/0/0)	3:00		x2		x2		x2
	(1/0/0)	3:00		x2		x2		x2
Half Kneeling Lat Pull				x8		x10		x12
				x8		x10		x12
				x8		x10		x12
Landmine				2x5		2x5		2x5
RFESS				x8		x10		x12
				x8		x10		x12
				x8		x10		x12
Partner Glute/Ham				x8		x10		x12
				x8		x10		x12
				x8		x10		x12
Wide Stance Anti-Rotation				2x8		2x8		2x8

Pre-Workout Stress:

Day 2	Tempo	Rest	Week 1	Reps	Week 2	Reps	Week 3	Reps
Bench Press	(1/0/0)	3:00		x2		x2		x2
	(1/0/0)	3:00		x2		x2		x2
	(1/0/0)	3:00		x2		x2		x2
	(1/0/0)	3:00		x2		x2		x2
Side Pank Cable Pull				3x8		3x10		3x12
SA OH Press				x5		x3		x10
				x5		x3		x10
				x5		x3		x10
Band W's				x8		x10		x12
				x8		x10		x12
				x8		x10		x12
Standing Band Sit Up				2x10		2x12		2x14
Deltoid Pulses				x8		x10		x12
				x8		x10		x12
				x8		x10		x12
Plank Pull				x8		x10		x10
				x8		x10		x10
				x8		x10		x10
SB SL Sea Saw				2x8		2x10		2x12

Pre-Workout Stress:								

Day 3	Tempo	Rest	Week 1	Reps	Week 2	Reps	Week 3	Reps
Loaded Squat Jumps	Exp	2:00		x5		x5		x5
				x5		x5		x5
				x5		x5		x5
Farmer's Walk				2x		2x		2x
Front Squat (50/55/60%)	(1/0/0)	2:00		x3		x3		x3
	(1/0/0)	2:00		x3		x3		x3
	(1/0/0)	2:00		x3		x3		x3
	(1/0/0)	2:00		x3		x3		x3
	(1/0/0)	2:00		x3		x3		x3
	(1/0/0)	2:00		x3		x3		x3
	(1/0/0)	2:00		x3		x3		x3
	(1/0/0)	2:00		x3		x3		x3
Wide Grip Chins				x8		x10		x12
				x8		x10		x12
				x8		x10		x12
TRX Palloff Press				2x8		2x8		2x8
Loaded Hip Lift				x8		x10		x12
				x8		x10		x12
				x8		x10		x12
DB Row				x8		x10		x12
				x8		x10		x12
				x8		x10		x12
Lunge Stance Lifts				2x8		2x8		2x8

Pre-Workout Stress:								

Day 4	Tempo	Rest	Week 1	Reps	Week 2	Reps	Week 3	Reps
Chain Bench (40/45/50%)	(1/0/0)	2:00		x3		x3		x3
	(1/0/0)	2:00		x3		x3		x3
	(1/0/0)	2:00		x3		x3		x3
	(1/0/0)	2:00		x3		x3		x3
	(1/0/0)	2:00		x3		x3		x3
	(1/0/0)	2:00		x3		x3		x3
	(1/0/0)	2:00		x3		x3		x3
	(1/0/0)	2:00		x3		x3		x3
TRX Triceps				2x8		2x10		2x12
Iron Cross				x8		x10		x12
				x8		x10		x12
				x8		x10		x12
Shoulder Scaption				x8		x10		x10
				x8		x10		x10
				x8		x10		x10
Get Up Progression 45 degree to bridge (pause)				2x3		2x4		2x5
BB Shrugs				x8		x10		x12
				x8		x10		x12
				x8		x10		x12
Ab Whee Roll Outs				x8		x10		x12
				x8		x10		x12
				x8		x10		x12
Standing Band Sit Up				2x8		2x10		2x12

Sample Block 1: Four times per week conjugate periodization for hockey players.

Program 4 (Advanced): Three Times per Week, Nonlinear, High/Low (Vertical Integration) Programming

Intensity is divided into high and low, maximizing the work-to-recovery relationship. High-intensity days consist of alactic development and submax/max weight training (85-100 percent 1RM), while low intensity serves to provide aerobic recovery and regeneration. Energy system intensity is kept below 74 percent to maximize recovery. Sunday is an off day. This program is modified for hockey players so that during the last block of the off-season, prior to training camp, moderate intensities are reintroduced to challenge the system to operate in the face of lactate and other metabolic by-products.

High	Low	High	Low	High	Low
Monday	Tuesday	Wednesday	Thursday	Friday	Saturday
Dynamic warm-up Speed Plyos Strength training: 75–80% + 1RM Front squat	x12 tempo runs Core work Recovery	Dynamic warm-up Speed Plyos Strength training 80–90% + 1RM Bench press	x12 tempo runs Core work Recovery	Dynamic warm-up Speed Plyos Strength training 85–95% + 1RM trap bar DL	Aerobic Circuit training

Sample Three-per-Week Block 1: High/low programming for hockey players. Although this model avoids the middle ground, these intensity ranges are important for hockey players to experience prior to training camp commencing. During the last block of training, programming specifically targets these ranges to challenge the system to perform in the face of metabolic buildup and increased acidity at the muscular level.

Program 5 (Advanced): Three Times per Week, Block Periodization

DSC
BORISOV STRENGTH & CONDITIONING

Block 1: Accumulation

Day 1	Tempo	Rest	WK1	G: +/-/=	Reps	WK 2	G: +/-/+=	Reps	WK 3	G: +/-/+=	Reps	WK 4	+/-/+	Reps	WK 5	+/-/+	Reps
Esculating Density (12 min)	(2/0/0)	No Rest			x5			x6			x5			x6			x5
A1.) Fat Bar Bench Press	(2/0/0)	No Rest			x5			x6			x5			x6			x5
								x6			x5			x6			x5
								x6			x5			x6			
A2.) Reverse Lunge	(2/0/0)				x5			x6			x5			x6			x5
	(2/0/0)				x5			x6			x5			x6			x5
								x6			x5			x6			x5
A3.) Ab Wheel Roll Out					3x5			3x5			3x5			3x5			3x5
Esculating Density (12 min)	(2/0/0)				x5			x6			x5			x6			x5
B1.) Snatch Grip RDL	(2/0/0)				x5			x6			x5			x6			x5
								x6			x5			x6			x5
B2.) Incline DB Press					x5			x6			x5			x6			x5
					x5			x5			x5			x5			x5
								x6			x6			x6			x5
B3.) Farmers Walk					x3			x3			x3			x3			x3

Day 2	Tempo	Rest	WK1	G: +/-/=	Reps	WK 2	G: +/-/+=	Reps	WK 3	G: +/-/+=	Reps	WK 4	+/-/+	Reps	WK 5	+/-/+	Reps
Esculating Density (12 min)	(2/0/0)	No Rest			x5			x6			x5			x6			x5
A1.) Fat Grip OH Press	(2/0/0)	No Rest			x5			x6			x5			x6			x5
								x6			x5			x6			x5
								x6						x6			
B1.) KB Row					x5			x6			x5			x6			x5
					x5			x6			x5			x6			x5
								x6			x5			x6			x5
B2.) Plank Pull					3x5			3x5			3x5			3x5			3x5
Esculating Density (12 min)	(2/0/0)				x5			x6			x5			x6			x5
C1.) Chin Ups	(2/0/0)				x5			x6			x5			x6			x5
								x6			x5			x6			x5
C2.) Landmine Row w/ Rouge ext					x5			x6			x5			x6			x5
					x5			x6			x5			x6			x5
								x6			x5			x6			x5
C3.) Kneeling Pallof Press					3x5			3x5			x3			x3			x3

Day 3	Tempo	Rest	WK1	G: +/-/=	Reps	WK 2	G: +/-/+=	Reps	WK 3	G: +/-/+=	Reps	WK 4	+/-/+	Reps	WK 5	+/-/+	Reps
Esculating Density (12 min)	(2/0/0)	No Rest			x6			x6			x5			x6			x5
A1.) Incline Fat Bar Bench	(2/0/0)	No Rest			x6			x6			x5			x6			x5
								x6			x5			x6			x5
								x6						x6			
A2.) RFESS	(2/0/0)				x5			x6			x5			x6			x5
	(2/0/0)				x5			x6			x5			x6			x5
								x6			x5			x6			x5
A3.) Ab Wheel Roll Out					3x5			3x5			3x5			3x5			3x5
Esculating Density (12 min)	(2/0/0)				x6			x6			x5			x6			x5
B1.) KB Hip Thrusters					x6			x6			x5			x6			x5
								x6			x5			x6			x5
B2.) Flat Bench Fly's	(2/0/0)				x10			x6			x5			x6			x5
	(2/0/0)				x10			x6			x5			x6			x5
								x6			x5			x6			x5
B3.) "Canninball" Farmers Walk					3x5			3x5			x3			x3			x3

Accumulation

213

Block 2: Transmutation (Max Strength)

Day 1	Tempo	Rest	WK1	G: +/-/=	Reps	WK 2	G: +/-/+=	Reps	WK 3	G: +/-/+=	Reps	WK 4	G:+/-/+=	Reps
A1.) BB Reverse Lunge	(2/1/0)	3:00			x8						x7			x6
	(2/1/0)	3:00			x6						x5			x4
					x4						x3			x2
					x4						x3			x2
					x6						x5			x4
					x8						x7			x6
A2.) Trap Bar Strict Press					x8						x5			x5
					x8						x5			x5
											x5			x5
B1.) BB SLDL		2:00			x8						x5			x5
		2:00			x8						x5			x5
											x5			x5
B2.) Shoulder Circuit					x8						x5			x5
					x8						x5			x5
											x5			x5
B3.) Garhammer Raise					3x5			3x5			3x5			3x5

Day 2	Tempo	Rest	WK1	G: +/-/+=	Reps	WK 2	G: +/-/+=	Reps	WK 3	G:+/-/+=	Reps	WK 4	G: +/-/+=	Reps
A1.) Incline Bench Press	(2/1/0)	3:00			x8			x8			x7			x6
	(2/1/0)	3:00			x6			x6			x5			x4
					x4						x3			x2
					x4						x3			x2
					x6			x6			x5			x4
					x8			x8			x7			x6
A2.) 1-Arm TRX Row w/offset KB					x8			x5			x6			x5
					x8			x5			x6			x5
								x5			x6			x5
B1.) SA Bench Press					x8			x5			x6			x5
					x8			x5			x6			x5
								x5			x6			x5
B2.) Fat Grip KB Row					x8			x5			x6			x5
					x8			x5			x6			x5
								x5			x6			x5

Day 3	Tempo	Rest	WK1	G: +/-/=	Reps	WK 2	G: +/-/+=	Reps	WK 3	G: +/-/+=	Reps	WK 4	G:+/-/+=	Reps
A1.) RFESS	(2/1/0)	3:00			x8			x8			x7			x6
	(2/1/0)	3:00			x6			x6			x5			x4
					x4						x3			x2
					x4						x3			x2
					x6			x6			x5			x4
					x8			x8			x7			x6
A2.) Candlestick Chin Ups					x8			x5			x6			x5
					x8			x5			x6			x5
								x5			x6			x5
B1.) KB Step Ups					x8			x5			x6			x5
					x8			x5			x6			x5
								x5			x6			x5
B2.) Straight Arm Lat Pull Down					x8			x5			x6			x5
					x8			x5			x6			x5
								x5			x6			x5

Transmutation

DSC
DONSKOV STRENGTH & CONDITIONING

Block 3: Realization (Power)														
Day 1	Tempo	Rest	WK1	G: +/-/=	Reps	WK 2	G: +/-/+=	Reps	WK 3	G: +/-/+=	Reps	WK 4	G:+/-/+=	Reps
A1.) Trap Bar DL w/chains	(1/0/0)	3:00			x5			x3			x3			x3
OR Deadlift	(1/0/0)	3:00			x5			x3			x3			x3
					x3			x3			x3			x3
A2.) Power Clean	Explosive	3:00			x3			x2			x2			x2
	Explosive	3:00			x3			x2			x2			x2
								x2			x2			x2
A3.) Trap Bar Jumps (15-20%)		3:00			x10			x10			x10			x10
		3:00			x10			x10			x10			x10
								x10			x10			x10
A4.) Depth Jumps		3:00			x10			x10			x10			x10
		3:00			x10			x10			x10			x10
								x10			x10			x10
A5.) Vertical Jump		3:00			:15			:15			:15			:15
		3:00			:15			:15			:15			:15
		3:00			:15			:15			:15			:15

Day 2	Tempo	Rest	WK1	G: +/-/=	Reps	WK 2	G: +/-/+=	Reps	WK 3	G: +/-/+=	Reps	WK 4	G:+/-/+=	Reps
A1.) Bench Press w/chains	(1/0/0)	3:00			x5			x3			x3			x3
	(1/0/0)	3:00			x5			x3			x3			x3
								x3			x3			x3
A2.) Push Press (Dip/dive/press)	Explosive	3:00			x3			x2			x2			x2
	Explosive	3:00			x3			x2			x2			x2
								x2			x2			x2
A3.) Elastic Push Up Depth Drop 6" Box		3:00			x10			x10			x10			x10
		3:00			x10			x10			x10			x10
								x10			x10			x10
A4.) Push Up Clap		3:00			x10			x10			x10			x10
		3:00			x10			x10			x10			x10
								x10			x10			x10
A5.) Seated MB Throw		3:00			x10			x10			x10			x10
		3:00			x10			x10			x10			x10
		3:00			x10			x10			x10			x10

Day 3	Tempo	Rest	WK1	G: +/-/=	Reps	WK 2	G: +/-/+=	Reps	WK 3	G: +/-/+=	Reps	WK 4	G:+/-/+=	Reps
A1.) Front Squat w/chains	(1/0/0)	3:00			x5			x3			x3			x3
OR Deadlift	(1/0/0)	3:00			x5			x3			x3			x3
								x3			x3			x3
A2.) Power Snatch	Explosive	3:00			x3			x2			x2			x2
	Explosive	3:00			x3			x2			x2			x2
								x2			x2			x2
A3.) Squat Jumps (15-20%)		3:00			x10			x10			x10			x10
		3:00			x10			x10			x10			x10
								x10			x10			x10
A4.) Hurdle Jumps		3:00			x8			x5			x6			x5
		3:00			x8			x5			x6			x5
								x5			x6			x5
A5.) Vertical Jump		3:00			:15			:15			:15			:15
		3:00			:15			:15			:15			:15
		3:00			:15			:15			:15			:15

Realization

Additional Considerations for Developing the Program

- Let the process run the plan, not the plan run the process.
- Programming should be malleable, moldable, and not set in stone. The micro should dictate the macro. Great coaches have a plan A and a plan B.
- Let your process, philosophy, and pedagogical principles dictate your program design.
- Continue to be a lifelong learner and allow your mistakes to become lessons to building better programs.
- There is no one best way to train.

- Allow the process to be cooperative in nature with the athlete. Top-down coaching may inhibit buy-in and program adherence.
- Future training should be broadly defined.
- Track everything.
- Learn from other coaches' mistakes.
- Design your program around a few fundamental concepts and exercises. Change as few variables at one time as possible. The fewer variables, the more one can predict biological adaptation.

Chapter 9

Short-Term Competition

Performance by the aggregation of marginal gains.
—Dave Brailsford

Short-term competitions, such as invite camps, special tournaments, and international play, pose several challenges to the performance staff. Among the variables that must be accounted for are travel, schedule (e.g., volume of practice and games in condensed time periods), performance testing, and regeneration methods, such as sleep, hydration, and nutrition. Although recovery and regeneration strategies should be a fabric of daily operations throughout the year, not all tournament rosters may adhere to this tenet. These small windows of time are critical in the education process and provide a platform for players to perform at optimal levels when it matters most. Maximal competition in minimal time frames is commonplace during short-term competition periods. In order for the performance staff to optimize these small windows, careful consideration of the following variables is necessary.

Three Variables of Performance on Demand

1. Travel

Travel, much like weight training, is a form of stress. Although not mechanical in nature, travel may cause physiological imbalances among the sympathetic and parasympathetic systems, dehydration, and psychological discomfort that may trigger the adrenals to overstimulate stress hormones. International flights, where multiple time zones are crossed, further complicate the issue, as jet lag, the detachment of the body's internal biological clock, is experienced. This can offset and alter the sleep/wake cycle, circadian rhythm, and hormones, such as cortisol and melatonin.

In addition, cabin pressure and humidity are kept low on most flights, which can result in excess fluid buildup in the tissues, known as edema. Travel places demands on the system and fatigue on the athlete and affects performance on the ice.

In order to avoid and offset these potential performance decrements, preplanning is necessary. The coach's job is to plan, initiate, review, and consistently improve the process of preparation, enabling the athlete to perform at the highest levels possible when it matters most. It is also the job of the performance team to educate the coaching staff and answer all questions pertaining to the plan. Interdisciplinary cooperation is key in developing short-term performance standards that can be replicated for future use. Several options exist to combat the stress of travel. The key is to have a working plan initiated prior to the short-term competition period and the travel leading up to initial departure. Travel planning may incorporate the following:

□ Hydration Plan—Cabin pressure and humidity may have negative effects on hydration levels, so it's imperative to rehydrate and avoid certain beverage selections during travel. Beverages such as cola, coffee, and energy drinks should be avoided because of the effects of caffeine on the adrenals and high sugar content on blood insulin levels. In addition, all beverages (with the exception of a few herbal teas), except water, act as diuretics that dehydrate the system. Water regulates a plethora of functions in the body, including the activity of the solutes (in vital organs and so on), the blood, and the transport of hormones and nutrients throughout the system. During long trips, international travel, and periods of extended stay, hydration levels are important to monitor.

Performance on Demand: Hydration

- Travel is a form of stress on the system.
- Proper planning is paramount during short-term competition periods.
- Never force an athlete to drink. Drink when thirsty.
- Water is an excellent option. It is nondiuretic and replenishes fluid imbalances experienced during travel.
- The body needs an absolute minimum of six to eight eight-ounce glasses of water per day.
- The best time to drink water is one glass thirty minutes before a meal and one two and a half hours after a meal.
- Adjusting water intake to mealtimes prevents the blood from becoming concentrated as a result of food intake. When the blood becomes concentrated, it draws water from the cells around it.[81]
- Avoid highly acidic beverages during travel, as these lower pH levels and promote water loss.
- Avoid caffeine. Caffeine stimulates the adrenals, increases stress-hormone release, increases cortisol levels, lowers pH, and tips the system in a sympathetic fight-or-flight state. Caffeine is also a diuretic and should be avoided in excessive amounts. The FDA currently states that 300 to 400 mg of caffeine each day is nonharmful. This equates to three six-ounce servings. During brief performance windows, hockey players should avoid excessive caffeine consumption.

- Compression Wear—Elastic molded body wear has become increasingly popular and proposes to "exert a pressure on the covered limbs to improve blood flow and reduce inflammation."[82] Several studies have shown benefits in reducing muscular soreness and enhanced restoration. These garments can also be worn during travel in order to prevent fluid buildup in the joints (edema) experienced during air travel and long road trips. The jury is still out as to the proposed benefits of compression wear as the perceived placebo effect may also cause a sense of enhanced recovery. Recovery tools, such as compression wear, may be used but should not be relied on as a significant form of regeneration.

◻ Time Zone Adaptation—Foreign travel is a difficult adjustment to the body. The circadian rhythm is altered. "These rhythms are measured by the distinct rise and fall of body temperature, plasma levels of certain hormones and other biological conditions. All of these are influenced by our exposure to sunlight and help determine when we sleep and when we wake."[83] Some excellent information on jet lag has been provided here courtesy of www.sleepfoundation.org.

  ○ Select a flight that allows early evening arrival and stay up until 10:00 p.m. local time. (If you must sleep during the day, take a short nap in the early afternoon but no longer than two hours. Set an alarm to be sure not to oversleep.)

  ○ Anticipate the time change for trips by getting up and going to bed earlier several days prior to an eastward trip and later for a westward trip.

  ○ Upon boarding the plane, change your watch to the destination time zone.

  ○ Avoid alcohol or caffeine at least three to four hours before bedtime. Both act as stimulants and prevent sleep.

  ○ Upon arrival at a destination, avoid heavy meals (a snack—not chocolate—is okay).

  ○ Avoid any heavy exercise close to bedtime. (Light exercise earlier in the day is fine.)

  ○ Bring earplugs and blindfolds to help dampen noise and block out unwanted light while sleeping.

  ○ Try to get outside in the sunlight whenever possible. Daylight is a powerful stimulant for regulating the biological clock. (Staying indoors worsens jet lag.)

◻ Contrary to popular belief, the types of foods we eat have no effect on minimizing jet lag.

Once travel is complete, the performance staff may monitor both resting heart rate and vertical jump numbers to see the impact travel has had on the nervous system. During subsequent days, these numbers may be reevaluated to ensure the athletes are adapting to the new time zone.

2. Performance Testing—Performance testing during short-term competition needs to be carefully planned by the performance staff. These periods typically consist of maximal on-ice competition with minimal downtime and place tremendous amounts of stress on the athletes involved, both physically and emotionally. The stress of travel, the psychological stress of making a tournament team, and the mechanical stress of on-ice performance may affect testing results and need to be thoroughly considered by the performance staff prior to creating testing protocol. Due to the demands and the overall volume of on-ice activity during this brief time window, lower-body strength testing and off-ice endurance testing are purposely avoided. Performance coaches may choose more activity-specific power and endurance tests. These are performed on the ice. Lower-body strength testing is avoided because of delayed muscle soreness, which may negatively affect competition in the following days.

Performance on Demand: Testing Protocol
Power
VJ / Broad Jump

The vertical jump or broad jump tests are easy to administer and provide immediate results to the performance staff regarding peak power output. To get a better understanding of power based on bodyweight the practitioner may also use the Sayers formula. The Sayers equation[84] estimates peak power output (peak anaerobic power output) from the vertical jump. A heavier athlete jumping the same height as a lighter individual has to do much more work to move and overcome a larger mass. This can be accounted for using the Sayers equation.

PAPw (Watts) = 60.7 jump height (cm) + 45.3 body mass (kg) - 2055

Upper-Body Strength
Bench Press

The bench press may be used to assess upper-body pushing strength. The practitioner instructs the athlete to load a weight that he or she can safely perform

221

five repetitions with. The coaching staff may take these numbers and calculate an approximate one-rep maximum using the Epley formula. W represents the weight in the bar, multiplied by R, the number of repetitions performed. This number is multiplied by .0333 and then added back to the original weight on the bar.

$$\text{Epley Formula: } (W*R*.0333) + W$$

For example, an athlete who performs the lift using 225 pounds for five repetitions would have an approximate one-rep maximum of 262 pounds. The Epley formula allows the practitioner to attain an approximate one-rep max without reaching threshold limits.

$$\text{One Rep Max: } (225 * 5 * .0333) + 225 = 262 \text{ lbs.}$$

Chin-Ups

Chin-ups can be used to test upper-body pulling strength. Depending on how the performance staff initiates testing protocol, general strength and strength endurance can be measured. General strength, nonspecific in nature, can be measured by limiting the total repetitions to five. In many cases of elite performers, this can be accomplished with the use of a weighted belt. An additional load of 25 to 45 pounds may be used for testing. If the goal is strength endurance, the ability to produce force over long periods of time, the test is administered using body weight for as many repetitions as possible. Both tests are good indicators of upper-body pulling but measure two different strength qualities.

General Strength: x 5 with additional weight (25 or 45lbs)
Strength Endurance: AMRAP (as many reps as possible)

Body Composition

The practitioner may use body composition measurements to assess the differences between lean mass and fat mass for each individual player. This can be done several ways, using different pieces of equipment. Underwater weighing currently provides one of the more accurate protocols in attaining these numbers. Fat is the only body constituent whose specific gravity is less than water. Players are weighed before and after entering the tub, and calculations are made accordingly. Skin calipers are also used to attain body composition numbers. The most important element during testing is consistency and making sure the tests are reliable and valid. The same individual, using the same sites, should test all athletes in attendance. Gender differences in body composition are common and should be accounted for. Elite male players typically fall between 10 and 12 percent, as opposed to elite female players who may fall slightly higher at 17 to 25 percent.

> Total Body Weight: 175
> % Body Fat: 12.2
> Lean Mass: 153.65
> Fat Mass: 21.35

Example: A 175-pound player with a body fat reading of 12.2 using the SkinDex calipers.

3. Regeneration
Sleep

Sleep may be the cheapest and most effective recovery tool for athletes of all sports. It is during sleep when the highest concentration of growth hormone is produced and parasympathetic tone is set. Sleep controls the secretion of several important hormones, such as melatonin and prolactin. Melatonin is released during sleep by the pineal gland in the brain and aids in the regulation of sleep-wake cycles. Prolactin is also released during sleep by the pituitary gland and controls appetite. Therefore sleep has a profound effect on eating, eating controls stress, and stress controls reproduction and performance gains. It is vitally important that athletes look to maximize sleep during times of intense competition schedule.

"In 1910, the average adult slept ten hours each night."[85] This number has slowly decreased each decade with the advent of technology, artificial light, diet, and overall poor sleeping habits. Today, that number looks more like 6.8 hours per night (Gallup Survey). Lack of sleep may affect performance in several different ways.

- Deprivation of sleep inhibits restoration by increasing inflammation and sympathetic nervous system activity.
- Short nights blunt the production of melatonin and lead to a cascade of hormonal events that can cause hypothalamic fatigue,

increased cortisol levels (high at night and low during the day), and altered insulin levels.

- Less prolactin is produced at night (at night means stronger natural killer and T cells) and more produced during the day. Prolactin during the day means autoimmunity and carbohydrate craving.
- The biggest problem with year-round short nights is that insulin will stay higher during the dark (when it should be flat) and cortisol falls too late so it won't come up early in the morning.[86]
- When cortisol is low in the morning, athletes will complain of fatigue, lack of motivation, and drowsiness.
- Lack of sleep also compromises immune function, as both melatonin and prolactin govern this system.

Tips for Sleeping

When you change the environment, the environment changes you.
—Law of Evolution

- Turn off all technology.
- Block any artificial light. Turn alarm clocks around, or unplug them. Cover up VCR/DSD lights, and invest in black-out blinds. Artificial light inhibits the production of melatonin and keeps the brain awake.
- Forbid adrenal-stimulating foods and drugs, especially coffee.
- Make a sleep schedule with a lights-out time. This establishes importance, and athletes can build their off-ice schedules around it.
- Reduce lifestyle stressors.
- Establish a sleep ritual. Athletes may not be able to control their sleep outcome, but they can control sleep behaviors and rituals. Warm showers, baths, light massages, and Jacuzzi time are all possible rituals. Select a preset time for lights out.
- Aim for eight to ten hours each night.

Nutrition

This does not have to be a lengthy, confusing subject. Nutrition is paramount in peak performance. Nutrition plays an important role in recovery, regeneration, and vitality. Athletes striving to gain a competitive edge place a high priority on nutrition and the foods and beverages they consume. Eating the wrong foods may alter performance, decrease energy, and cause blood sugar levels to fluctuate in an irregular fashion. During short-term competition, the performance staff is responsible for postgame snacks, postgame meals, and beverage selection. Following a few simple rules can make the food-selection process relatively easy.

Tips for Food Selection

- Avoid C.R.A.P. Stay away from carbohydrates, refined foods, additives, and preservatives. You will find most all of these items in the middle of the grocery store. They are prepackaged and have very long shelf lives. Eat real F.O.O.D.—fruits and vegetables, organic lean proteins, omega-three fatty acids, and drink plenty of water.
- Eat protein with each meal. The fewer legs the better (fish, chicken, and beef). One serving is equal to the palm of your hand with your fingers spread.
- Eat vegetables with each meal. Vegetables are nutrient-dense foods, which means they have a lot of vitamins and minerals in their composition. One serving is equal to the size of a fist.
- Eat breakfast every day; breakfast kick-starts the metabolism. Blood sugar levels are low, and cortisol levels should be high in the morning. The body is preparing to break the overnight fast.
- Drink single-ingredient beverages. Water is the number-one beverage of choice. Most all other beverages act as diuretics that rid the body of water. In addition, sugary and caffeinated beverages cause fluctuation of blood sugar levels and stimulate the adrenals, which may eventually lead to hypoglycemia.
- Eat healthy fats. Lean cuts of meat, olive oil, flax seed, fish oil, avocados, and nuts are all excellent options. Fat is a very important constituent in a healthy diet. Saturated fats may also be consumed. Saturated fats increase HDL (the good cholesterol) while also increasing LDL (the bad cholesterol); however, there are different sizes of LDL, the small particles being the most harmful. Saturated fats are currently shown to decrease these small particles.[87] Serving size is equal to one thumb.

▫ Postgame protein shake! Whey protein has a great profile of essential amino acids; these are amino acids (proteins) that cannot be made inside the body and must come from a balanced diet. EEAs are about half of all whey protein amino acids. In particular, whey contains a greater amount of the BCAA leucine. It is now well accepted that leucine acts as a signaling molecule for muscle growth. Whey protein tastes great and is absorbed quickly. Recent research has shown that the body can utilize only about ten grams of EEA from twenty grams of whey protein, at any one time. This is known as the "muscle full" effect.[88]

Pregame Meal (Three or More Hours before Game)

This should be a meal that consists of a nonfired protein and vegetable source. Foods, such as fish, chicken, vegetables (peppers, broccoli), and a loaded salad are all good choices. Make wise carbohydrate choices at this time. An easy way to remember good options is the phrase: "Think whole-grain, brown and grown close to the ground." These foods are nutrient dense and have a minimal impact on blood sugar levels. Serving size should be the size of a cupped palm. Foods that elevate blood sugar levels (e.g., white bread, white pasta, and white potatoes) should be avoided. These foods are empty calories (minimal nutrients). The postgame meal should look very similar, as these foods serve as the foundation of healthy eating and elevated performance.

Immediately After Game

Replenish (refuel), repair (protein), and rehydrate (water). This is a great time for a postgame protein shake with additional carbohydrates.

Traveling Snacks

Have a plan, work the plan, and plan for the unexpected. Snacks during travel may consist of trail mix (no chocolate), veggies, fresh fruit, almond butter, whole-grain bagels, mixed nuts, beef jerky, sports bars (Power Crunch, Balance, Dale's Raw Bars), and low-fat Greek yogurt. These items can be purchased at the grocery store prior to departure or along the way. When it comes to snacks, avoid words such as *creamy, spicy,* and *fried*.

Biological Individuality

From a structural and biochemical standpoint, not all bodies are created equal. Although following basic food recommendations may set hockey players up for success, certain body types may be able to thrive consuming variable portions of macronutrients. "While the same physical mechanisms and the same metabolic processes are operating in all human bodies, the structures are sufficiently diverse and the genetically determined enzyme efficiencies vary sufficiently from individual to individual so that the sum total of all the reactions taking place in one individual's body may be very different from those taking place in the body of another individual at the same age, sex, and body size. When we pay attention to differences—anatomical, physiological, and biochemical—we are inevitably led to consider differences in nutritional needs."[89]

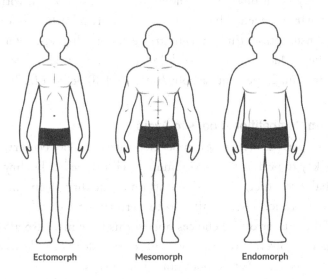

Ectomorph   Mesomorph   Endomorph

Ectomorph versus mesomorph versus endomorph

Ectomorphs

These players are naturally thin and may struggle to gain weight. Ectomorphs are hard gainers and need to work very hard to see improvements in body composition. Ectomorphs should eat a well-balanced diet but may be a little looser with dietary rules, especially carbohydrates. Macronutrient breakdown may look as follows 25 percent protein, 55 percent carbohydrates, and 20 percent fat.[90]

Mesomorph

Mesomorphs typically have very athletic bodies, lean mass, and medium bone structure. Mesomorphs do well with a balanced composed of 30 percent protein, 40 percent carbohydrates, and 30 percent fat.[91]

Endomorph

Endomorphs typically are larger-framed athletes who carry additional mass. Endomorphs do not do well with sugar and need to be cognizant and aware of carbohydrate consumption. Endomorphs are better on a higher-protein diet. Macronutrient breakdown is roughly 35 percent protein, 25 percent carbohydrates, and 40 percent fat.[92]

Short-Term Competition: Foods to Avoid

During periods of intense competition with minimal recovery, "working in" is the key to performing at optimum levels on the ice. Fueling properly with a balanced diet, focusing on attaining quality sleep, and making the right hydration choices all lead to performing well when it matters most. Making poor off-ice choices during this time may also affect on-ice performance, however, in a negative context. In order to avoid this outcome, hockey players should avoid poor nutrition choices.

- Caffeine—There has been research to show that caffeine may actually improve short-term performance.[93] It has been suggested that caffeine may enhance time to fatigue by way of "postulated metabolic effect of slowing the rate of muscle glycogen use." Indeed, caffeine stimulates the release of a variety of CNS neurotransmitters, including catecholamines and cortisol. The issue with caffeine use is its abuse. Overconsumption (more than 300 to 400mg, or three six-ounce cups of coffee) can fatigue the adrenals, placing the athlete in a constant fight-or-flight response, eventually leading to fatigue and compromised blood sugar.

◻ Coffee is also a strong oxidant, greatly increasing oxidation within the cells. Simply put, this causes you to age faster.[94]

◻ Avoid alcohol. Alcohol is a naked carbohydrate; it does not offer any nutritional value. It is extremely refined (more refined than white sugar), forcing cells to make energy rapidly. This causes shifts in blood sugar, eventually leading to hypoglycemia.

◻ Processed and packaged food, such as white bread, sugar, and many types of pasta are empty calories and do not offer nutritional value because they lack essential vitamins and minerals.

◻ Eat often. Prolonging the time between meals may tax the adrenals because the lower the blood sugar levels, the more cortisol it takes to normalize them. The goal should be to eat every two to three hours.

A Summer Strength and Conditioning Guide for Parents: Three Pitfalls to Avoid

It's about that time of year again! A time where youth athletes are finishing up their competitive seasons and looking forward to the summer. It's also a time when parents are looking at enlisting the service of a personal trainer or strength coach to aid in the athletic development of their children. This is a big decision for a parent and warrants a little homework. After all, you wouldn't give your hard-earned money to an investment banker without knowing his or her background, philosophy, and practical experience. The same can be said for physical conditioning. Health is the most important investment of all, and to place it in the hands of a competent coach takes a little investigating. The following are three pitfalls to avoid when choosing where your son or daughter will train this summer.

1. Early Specialization

Save your money! Young children under the age of twelve do not need to be exposed to a systemic, comprehensive strength and conditioning plan. Save your money and play multiple sports. That's right! Play baseball, lacrosse, soccer, rugby, or basketball. This aids in the development of physical literacy, and when it's finally time to send your child to a competent strength coach, you will make his or her job *much* easier. Much of the problem with today's youth athletes is that they don't know how to *move*!

Movement literacy is knowledge of foundational human movement, such as kicking, jumping, throwing, receiving, catching, bounding, tumbling, and skipping, which serve as a foundational prerequisites for advanced activity.

During early development, multiple exposures to various movement capacities allow young children to learn authentically without preprogrammed, memorized response. Physical literacy increases the database of the human nervous system. Elements, such as balance, agility, coordination, and basic motor control, can be gained while playing and having *fun*. "If fundamental motor skill development is not developed between the ages of 8–11 and 9–12 for females and males, a significant window of opportunity has been lost."[95] Bottom line: get moving, the less structure the better!

Think of physical literacy as a big, oversized umbrella. As strength coach and therapist Darcy Norman states, "A person with a large surface area umbrella of protection made of mobility, stability, and strength is able to move freely under the umbrella without getting wet." There would be a lot less chronic injury in today's youth if movement preceded year-round training.

2. Randomness—Avoid it like the plague. Everyone should have a plan! Let's go back to our investment guy. You would never give your money to a person with no plan, no strategy, and no tracking measure. The sad thing is this happens *all* the time in the training world. Workouts of the day, planned randomness, and the inability to track progress are all red flags to well-established strength practitioners. Great coaches have a plan A and a plan B, track progress, and are willing to manipulate. They always, always, always have a plan.

3. Specific programs—99.9 percent of youth athletes don't need a *speed*-specific program, an *agility*-specific program, or an *endurance*-specific program. The truth is they need to get *strong*! Strength is the bedrock, the foundation upon which all other abilities are reliant. Get strong! No excuses. Strength is not a specialized motor ability; it's general in nature. Players should not be standing a BOSU ball, blindfolded, with a hockey stick in their hands. This is not strength training. There are many qualities that cannot be overloaded on the ice, and strength is one of them. Find a program that balances basic patterns of push, pull, knee-dominant, and hip-dominant activities. Wash, rinse, and repeat!

I believe that strength training does not need to be as specific to the sporting action as some suggest. Speed training needs to have a greater degree of specificity than strength training, and the energy system training has the greatest need of all three for specificity. —Ian King

General ←--→ **Specific**
Strength Training   Speed Training   Endurance Training

There are many other pitfalls that parents may fall into when deciding where to send their son or daughter for the summer. The important thing is to ask questions and look for coaches who have practical experience and knowledge and provide results. Searching for a strength coach is a process, just like finding an investment banker, except now the most important investment of all is on the line—health!

Strength Training for Hockey: Three Qualities often Overlooked during the Off-Season

The sport of hockey is extremely demanding. Players reaching speeds of up to thirty miles per hour is equivalent to hundreds of small car crashes occurring throughout the course of a seven- to eight-month season. Physiological, psychological, and mechanical stressors mount during this time. Strength and conditioning practitioners face a major challenge: the law of competing demands. Practitioners must balance stress so that players perform optimally when it matters most on the ice. This job changes during the off-season when the major stressors of competition are removed. The off-season, although brief, is critically important for physical preparation and the application of additional stressors that may not be appropriate during the period of intense competition.

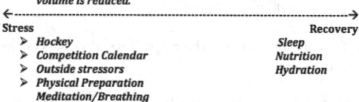

> *Stress experienced on the ice = < stress in the weight room*
> *< Stress experienced on the ice = > stress in the weight room*

In-Season stress/recovery: The goal is to manage this relationship and create balance so that players may perform on the ice during competitive periods. Physical preparation, training frequency, and overall training volume is reduced.

←---→

Stress   **Recovery**
- ➤ *Hockey*   *Sleep*
- ➤ *Competition Calendar*   *Nutrition*
- ➤ *Outside stressors*   *Hydration*
- ➤ *Physical Preparation*
  Meditation/Breathing

Off-Season stress/recovery: The goal is to manage this relationship and create balance, however, the major source of "stress" has now changed. Physical preparation, training frequency and overall volume are increased.

←---→

Stress   **Recovery**
- ➤ *Physical Preparation*   *Sleep*
- ➤ *Outside Stressors*   *Nutrition*
                                          Hydration
                                          Meditation/Breathing

The law of competing demands during the in-season and off-season for the competitive hockey player.

The following are three qualities often overlooked during the off-season/preparation period for hockey players. I believe these qualities are crucial for continued athletic development, efficiency, and sustainability.

Position: Posterior Pelvic Tilt / Internal Rotation of the Ribs

Any machine, including the human body, operating in poor position leads to a decreased efficiency, increased demand in fuel to accomplish common tasks, and an increase in the possibility of chronic overload. Poor position is the equivalent of riding a bike with a rusty chain. It may take you across the finish line, but efficiency and structural integrity are compromised and in the long run, mechanical breakdown is inevitable. Hockey is played in a flexed-hip position, placing both concentric and isometric stress on the hips and quadriceps during long-duration force application. The specificity of this mechanical position places postural adaptation on the player, facilitating certain muscle synergists and inhibiting or turning off others. If the hip flexors are constantly facilitated, there is a high probability that the pelvis will be pulled into an anteriorly tipped position. This may cause impingement and mechanical issues within the joint. The practitioner may think of the hip joint as the shoulder joint of the lower body. An anteriorly tipped scapula immediately places the humeral head in a compromised position. Ron Hruska, founder of the Postural Restoration Institute (PRI), sums it up eloquently: "Is an acetabulum over a femur any different than an acromion process over a humeral head?"

Solution

A solution to the anterior, malpositioned pelvis is to create adjacent stiffness of the anterior core musculature and facilitate the hamstrings. This serves to stiffen adjacent structures and reposition the pelvis posteriorly, thereby taking pressure and pull off of the tight, overactive hip musculature. "It is reasonable to think that if these lengthened muscles are activated, thereby resetting the length tension relationship of the muscle spindles, the muscles on the opposite side of the system would begin to let go."[96] One of my favorite, simple-to-use resets is the 90/90 balloon breathing technique, used by PRI. This exercise posteriorly tilts the pelvis, engaging the hamstring musculature, while simultaneously internally rotating the ribs, allowing for optimal diaphragm function and abdominal support. This position facilitates muscles that are often inhibited because of the mechanics of the hockey stride.

Used with Permission from the Postural Restoration
Institute www.posturalrestoration.com[97]

Strength Training: "The Conversion Block"

Hockey players are not Olympic lifters, power lifters, or hundred-meter sprinters. Although variations of all sporting elements are used in the training process, the coach's goal should always be to move from general to specific in nature. Hockey players need both strength and power *but* must be able to sustain these qualities during the course of competition for success on the ice.

Many coaches periodize strength by focusing first on accumulation (general strength) and then max strength, followed by power. The problem with the power conversion phase is that speeds in the weight room fail to replicate those experienced on the ice. The late, great sprint coach Charlie Francis echoed these thoughts with regard to weight training implications and the power conversion phase for elite sprinters. He states, "I also eliminated the traditional 'conversion phase' which sprint coaches had adopted to bring velocities in weight-lifting closer to the sprint speed. I concluded that sprinters' extremities moved so much faster in running than in lifting that any increase in lifting speed was irrelevant." This is true for hockey players as well, as velocities on the ice may reach upward of thirty miles per hour, much greater than those experienced in the weight room while under load.

Solution

These implications have led me to periodize the conversion block by focusing on strength endurance, or what Tudor Bompa refers to as *muscle endurance*.[98] The goal is simple; slowly move from general to specific so that the player is ready for the demands of the season at the correct moment in the training process. This is accomplished by decreasing intensity and rest, increasing volume, and challenging the athlete to contract appropriate musculature in the presence of lactate accumulation. The power phase has been replaced with the strength-endurance phase. This phase leads the player directly into training camp and is most specific to the demands of the game.

Preparatory		Competitive		Transition
GPP	SPP	Pre-comp	Main Comp	Transition

Strength	Accumulation/ Max Strength	Conversion -Power -Muscle Endurance	Maintenance	Regeneration
Endurance	Aerobic Endurance	Foundation of Specific Endurance	Specific Endurance	Aerobic Endurance
Speed	Aerobic Endurance/Anaerobic Endurance	Foundation of Speed	Specific Speed/Agility	

Bompa, 1993: The periodization of main bio motor abilities (3)
This table depicts the periodization of multiple bio-motor abilities during each block (usually 4-6 weeks) of training. Strength training is slowly converted to strength endurance or power for hockey players. Careful consideration should be taken during this time as velocities in the weight room fail to replicate those on the ice. Aerobic endurance is slowly converted into sport specific anaerobic endurance and speed/acceleration is slowly progressed into application specific acceleration.

Energy System Development: "Working the V"

"The average player plays between 12 and 20 shifts per game and has an average rest period of 225 seconds between shifts (Wise, 1993). The rest interval between periods is fifteen minutes. It has been estimated that 70% to 80% of the energy for a hockey athlete is derived from the alactic and lactic systems."[99] This does not take away from the importance of aerobic development, as these adaptations act as favorable prerequisites for higher-intensity work, while simultaneously giving the players time away from the grind and extended recovery needed when training under lactate anaerobiosis. Chasing the energy system is the same as chasing pain. Many times, the problem is the efficiency of the supporting structures and pathways. One of the biggest mistakes I made as a coach was to constantly tax the lactic system too early and too often. This is a system that adapts and plateaus relatively quickly and causes maximal metabolic disturbance. Coach Frank Dick defines strength endurance, as "training to develop the athletes' ability to apply force in the climate of lactic anaerobiosis." He further warns, "Strength endurance training causes considerable wear and tear in the athletes' organism, and it is possible that a saturation of microcycles with units of this type would cause a loss of mental and physical resilience."[100]

Solution

Working the V—Both aerobic and alactic systems are trained first, the former as a supply and recovery system, the latter as a system that provides immediate ATP for explosive effort. Both systems are taxed without the buildup of acidosis. The anaerobic lactate system is trained during later blocks of the training plan, preparing the player for the demands of training camp. This is known as what strength Coach Mike Robertson refers to as "working the V." Working the V simply means working opposite ends of the continuum and slowly progressing toward middle ground; the longer the off-season, the more obtuse the angle and the wider the V. Short off-season periods produce the opposite effect, acute angles, and a much narrower V. As the V slowly narrows, training shifts to more lactate work building up to training camp and the regular season. This shifts priority toward energy demands that have a strong correlation to sporting demands. The peripheral adaptations of the lactate system are trained approximately three to six weeks prior to the commencement of training camp.

There you have it. Three programming qualities often overlooked for competitive hockey players. Positioning, the conversion block, and working the V are elements that we at Donskov Strength and Conditioning think are very important when training our unique population of athletes.

300-Yard Shuttle for Ice Hockey: To Test or not to Test?

I've been involved in the game of hockey my entire life, first as a player and now as a strength coach. I remember the demands of testing, the competition amongst teammates and the feeling of self-satisfaction after the effort of exertion. Testing was, and still is a rewarding time for me. Looking back, one protocol that has stood the test of time, both past and present, in the sport of ice hockey is the 300-yard shuttle. I endured this test for many years as a player, and have had it in my coaching arsenal during testing day to see "who was in shape" and ready for the demands of a long, drawn out, grinding season packed with 30mph collisions and large amounts of travel. However, just like everything else in the biological sciences, the more you learn, the more you question yourself, the more you question your methods, the more you question common practice. After all common practice doesn't always equate to best practice. Below are three reasons we no longer test the 300-yard shuttle at DSC.

1) **The demands of the game:** Watch the player, not the game. The best players on the ice are cerebral competitors with elite skill set. They "think" the game at high levels and are masters of energy expenditure. In other words they are efficient. Efficiency is the cost of output relative to input. Hockey is a game of intermittent acceleration, deceleration, change of direction, strength, power, and capacity. Shifts are kept short and contain 45 to 60 seconds of work characterized by short, two-second accelerations followed by coasting and decelerations of about 2.1 seconds. [1] Rarely, if ever, does a player skate full speed during a shift. We cannot simply equate a sixty-second shuttle to a typical hockey shift. The bioenergetics simply don't match up. The former is a combination of alactic aerobic qualities; the latter is a lactate endeavor. I am not suggesting that the lactate system is not important for the hockey playing community, but it is my opinion that it is over programmed and oversaturated during large portions of the off-season and sadly

239

even during the season. This comes at a physiological cost, as this form of work is grueling, taxing and compromising to recovery.

2) **Programming:** I had the opportunity to listen to my friend Doug Kechijian lecture a few weeks ago. Doug is an extremely bright physical therapist/strength coach and co founder of Resilient Physical Therapy in New York. During his lecture Doug made a comment that stuck in my head, he said "only test things that will influence your program." It was a reassuring moment for me. We don't test the 300-yard shuttle anymore because it doesn't have a major influence on our programming. In fact it's a very small piece. The majority of our programming comes from working opposite ends of the energy system continuum. We call it working the V.

ESD Continuum

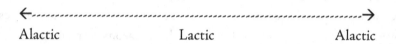

Alactic   Lactic   Alactic

Working the V—Both aerobic and alactic systems are trained first, the former as a supply and recovery system, and the latter as a system that provides immediate ATP for explosive effort. Both systems are taxed without the buildup of acidosis. The anaerobic lactate system is trained during later blocks of the training plan, preparing the player for the demands of training camp. This is known as what strength Coach Mike Robertson refers to as "working the V." It simply means working opposite ends of the continuum and slowly progressing toward middle ground; the longer the off-season, the more obtuse the angle and the wider the V. Short off-season periods produce the opposite effect, acute angles, and a much narrower V. As the V slowly narrows, training shifts to more lactate work building up to training camp and the regular season. The peripheral adaptations of the lactate system are trained approximately three to six weeks prior to the commencement of training camp. The majority of our summer is spent training alactic and aerobic qualities. Why? The lactic system adapts and plateaus relatively quickly, which leads to point three.

3) **Time course of adaptation of the lactic system:** The lactate system plateaus and adapts relatively quickly. [2,3,4,5] The time course for the enzymatic adaptations in glycolytic kinetics, such as an increase in phosphorylase, hexokinase, and phosphofructinase do not take nearly as long as adaptations that affect structural proteins, such as increase in myofibrils, mitochondrial density, and cardiac volume. One particular study that champions the use of anaerobic, lactate training in the often-cited Tabata study *"Effects of moderate-intensity endurance and high-intensity intermittent training on anaerobic capacity and ˙VO2max."* [6] When one digs deeper into the research, the study actually reveals just how quickly one can harness these adaptations. The study tracked two groups of seven moderately trained individuals for six weeks. Groups were broken down as follows:

Moderate Intensity Endurance:
Protocol: 60-minute workout at 70%VO2max/5xweek.
Results: Anaerobic capacity (as judged by the maximal accumulated oxygen deficit) did not increase significantly, but VO2 increased by 5 ml·kg^{-1}·min^{-1}

High Intensity Exercise Group:
Protocol: :20 on/: 10 x 7-8 sets at 170% VO2max/5 days/week. 1-day/week subjects exercised for 30 min @70% VO2.
Results: Anaerobic capacity increased 23% after 4 weeks of training, 28% after 6 weeks. VO2 increased 7 ml·kg^{-1}·min^{-1}

So why is this important for coaches training athletes? Take look at the Tabata group, they increased anaerobic capacity a total of 28% in six weeks. That's fantastic progress in a very short time frame. In addition, after week four they only made a 5% increase in anaerobic capacity. Adaptation started to plateau. Bottom line, in about six weeks, one can make significant improvements in the lactic system. That's great news coaches. So why do we feel the need to train this system year round?

Our Solution

We test what we train. We spend the majority of the off-season training top end acceleration/speed and sprinkle in bouts of aerobic work during recovery. Our goal is to measure power output and the ability to repeat performance. In order to assess this, we use a repeat sprint test. Repeat sprint ability is characterized by short-duration sprints (less than ten seconds) interspersed with brief recovery periods (usually less than sixty seconds). Anaerobic glycolysis supplies approximately 40 percent of the total energy during a single six-second sprint, but this number shifts toward aerobic contribution as the number of sprints increase. [7]

The coach places two cones twenty meters (sixty-five feet) apart. The athlete performs ten total sprints (or more) every thirty seconds. Coaches may also choose to cut the distance in half and use a shuttle format. The coach documents best time, average time, and the fatigue index. The fatigue index for running is calculated as follows:

$$FI \text{ (running)} = \frac{100 \times (S \text{ slowest} - S \text{ fastest})}{S \text{ fastest}} \text{ [8]}$$

OR

To take in consideration of all sprints (not just fastest and slowest), the coach may use a speed decrement formula. [8]

$$Sdec \text{ (\%)} = 100 \times \frac{(S1+S2+S3+S4....\text{final})}{S1 \times \text{number of sprints}} \text{ [8]}$$

By no means are these the only conditioning tests, but we have been using them the past year with relative success. As our level of knowledge continues to grow so does the protocol, testing procedures and hopefully our results. I think it's important to constantly question, seek answers and never be satisfied because it's always been done a certain way. It is our job as coaches to challenge fixed ideas derived from long established practice and to control our biased minds. I attempt to do this daily, as my goal is to constantly seek better answers for our athletic populations.

References:

H. Green, P. Bishop, M. Houston, R. McKillop, and Norman, "Time, Motion, and Physiological

[2] B. McKay, D. Paterson, and J. Kowalchuck, "Effect of Short-Term High-Intensity Training Versus Continuous Training on O_2 Uptake Kinetics, Muscle Deoxygenation, and Exercise Performance," *J Appl. Physiol.* 107 (May 14, 2009):128–138

[3] K. Burgomaster, N. Cermak, S. Phillips, C. Benton, A. Bonen, and M. Gibala, "Divergent Response of Metabolite Transport Proteins in Human Skeletal Muscle after Sprint Interval Training and Detraining," *Am. J. Physiol. Regul. Integr. Comp. Physiol.* 292 (2007): R1970–R1976

[4] K. A. Burgomaster, K. R. Howarth, S. M. Phillips, M. Rakobowchuck, M. J. Macdonald, S. L. McGee, and M. J. Gibala, "Similar Metabolic Adaptations during Exercise after Low Volume Sprint Interval and Traditional Endurance Training in Humans," *J. Physiol* 586 no. 1 (2008): 151–160

[5] K. A. Burgomaster, S. C. Hughes, G. J. Heigenhauser, S. N. Bradwell, and M. J. Gibala, "Six Sessions of Sprint Interval Training Increases Muscle Oxidative Potential and Cycle Endurance Capacity in Humans," *J. Appl. Physiol.* 98 no. 6 (2005): 1985–1990.

[6] Tabata, I. et al. (1996). Effects of Moderate-intensity endurance and high-intensity intermittent training on anaerobic capacity and V02max. *Journal of the American College of Sports Med* 28(10): 1327-1330.

[7] Gaitanos, G., Williams, C., Boobis, L. & Brooks, S. (1993). Human muscle metabolism during intermittent maximal exercise. *Journal of Applied Physiology* 75(2): 712-719.

[8] M. Cardinale, R. Newton, and N. Kazunori, "Strength and Conditioning Biological Principles and Practical Applications" (John Wiley and Sons, 2011).

Notes

Chapter 1

1   H. Green, P. Bishop, M. Houston, R. McKillop, and Norman, "Time, Motion, and Physiological Assessments of Ice Hockey Performance," *Journal of Applied Physiology* 40 no. 2 (1976): 159–163.

2   Bompa T. "Theory and Methodology of Training" Kendall/Hunt Pub. Co; 3rd edition (1994).

3   T. Rhodes and P. Twist, *The Physiology of Ice Hockey* (University of British Columbia).

4   Modified from I. King, "Foundations of Physical Preparation" (King Sport Publishing, 2005).

5   Montgomery, DL., "Physiological Profile of Professional Hockey Players—A Longitudinal Comparison," *Applied Physiology and Nutrition* 31 no. 3 (2006): 181–5.

Chapter 2

6   "Long-Term Athletic Development," Canadian Sport for Life (Canadian Sport Centres, 2010).

7   Ibid.

8   F. Dick, *Sport Training Principles* (Lepus Books, 2013).

9   K. Ericsson. "The Role of Deliberate Practice in the Acquisition of Expert Preformance," *Phycological Review* Vol 100. No. 3, 363-406, 1993.

10 Hockey Canada, "Long-Term Player Development Plan: Hockey for Life," Hockey for Excellence.

11 J. Drabik, *Children and Sports Training* (Stadion Publishing Company, 1996).

12 H. Green, P. Bishop, M. Houston, R. McKillop, and R. Norman, "Time, Motion, and Physiological Assessments of Ice Hockey Performance," *Journal of Applied Physiology* 40 no. 2 (1976): 159–163.

13 J. Joyce and D. Lewindon, "High Performance Training for Sports," *Human Kinetics* (2014).

Chapter 3

14 G. Cook, "Athletic Body in Balance," *Human Kinetics* (2003).

15 Ibid.

16 Ibid.

17 Kiesel et al. "Can Serious injury in Professional football be predicted by a preseason functional movement screen?" *North Am J Sports Phys Ther* 2007: 2: 147-158.

18 Gaitanos, G., Williams, C., Boobis, L. & Brooks, S. (1993). Human muscle metabolism during intermittent maximal exercise. *Journal of Applied Physiology* 75(2): 712-719.

19 J. Joyce and D. Lewindon, *"High Performance Training for Sports,"* Human Kinetics (2014).

20 Cook, G, *Athletic Body in Balance,* Human Kinetics, 2003.??

Chapter 4

21 T. Bompa and D. Chambers, *Total Hockey Conditioning* (Firefly Books, 2003).

22 P. Twist and T. Rhodes, *The Physiology of Ice Hockey,* Sports Science, University of British Columbia.

23 The Canadian Hockey Association. Source: *Intermediate Level Manual* (1989), 11.10.)

24 F. Dick, *Sport Training Principles* (Lepus Books, 2013).

25 Shelle Lau, Kris Berg, Richard W. Latin, and John Noble, "Comparison of Active and Passive Recovery of Blood Lactate and Subsequent Performance of Repeated Work Bouts in Ice Hockey Players," *Journal of Strength and Conditioning Research* 15 no. 3 (2001): 367–371.

26 H. Green, P. Bishop, M. Houston, R. McKillop, and R. Norman, "Time, Motion, and Physiological Assessments of Ice Hockey Performance," *Journal of Applied Physiology* 40 no. 2 (1976): 159–163.

27 Shelle Lau, Kris Berg, Richard W. Latin, and John Noble, "Comparison of Active and Passive Recovery of Blood Lactate and Subsequent Performance of Repeated Work Bouts in Ice Hockey Players," *Journal of Strength and Conditioning Research* 15 no. 3 (2001): 367–371.

28 M. Hargreaves and L. Spriet, "Exercise Metabolism," *Human Kinetics* (2006).

29 R. Maughan and M. Gleeson, *Biochemical Basis for Sport* (Oxford University Press Inc., 2010).

30 B. McKay, D. Paterson, and J. Kowalchuck, "Effect of Short-Term High-Intensity Training Versus Continuous Training on O_2 Uptake Kinetics, Muscle Deoxygenation, and Exercise Performance," *J Appl. Physiol.* 107 (May 14, 2009):128–138; K. Burgomaster, N. Cermak, S. Phillips, C. Benton, A. Bonen, and M. Gibala, "Divergent Response of Metabolite Transport Proteins in Human Skeletal Muscle after Sprint Interval Training and Detraining," *Am. J. Physiol. Regul. Integr. Comp. Physiol.* 292 (2007): R1970–R1976; K. A. Burgomaster, K. R. Howarth, S. M. Phillips, M. Rakobowchuck, M. J. Macdonald, S. L. McGee, and M. J. Gibala, "Similar Metabolic Adaptations during Exercise after Low Volume Sprint Interval and Traditional Endurance Training in Humans," *J. Physiol* 586 no. 1 (2008): 151–160; K. A. Burgomaster, S. C. Hughes, G. J. Heigenhauser, S. N. Bradwell, and M. J. Gibala, "Six Sessions of Sprint Interval

Training Increases Muscle Oxidative Potential and Cycle Endurance Capacity in Humans," *J. Appl. Physiol.* 98 no. 6 (2005): 1985–1990.

31 M. Cardinale, R. Newton, and N. Kazunori, "Strength and Conditioning Biological Principles and Practical Applications" (John Wiley and Sons, 2011).

32 F. Hatfield, *Power: A Scientific Approach* (Contemporary Books, 1989).

33 D. MacDougall and D. Sale, "Continuous Vs. Interval Training: A Review for the Athlete and Coach," *Can Journal of Applied Sports Science* 6 no. 2 (1981): 93–7.

34 B. Noonan, "Intragame Blood Lactate Values during Ice Hockey and Their Relationships to Commonly Used Hockey Testing Protocols," *J Strength Cond Res*, 24 no. 9 (2010): 2290–5.

35 F. Dick, *Sport Training Principles* (Lepus Books, 2013).

36 Ibid.

37 Ibid.

38 J. Jamieson, *Ultimate MMA Conditioning* (Performance Sports Inc., 2009).

39 J. Jamieson, *Ultimate MMA Conditioning* (Performance Sports Inc., 2009).

40 F. Dick, *Sport Training Principles* (Lepus Books, 2013).

41 T. Bompa, *Theory and Methodology of Training* (Kendall/Hunt Publishing Company, 1994).

42 J. Blatherwick, *Over-Speed Skill Training for Hockey* (The Publishing Group, USA Hockey, 1992).

43 V. Issurin, *Block Periodization 2* (Ultimate Athlete Concepts, USA, 2008).

44 M. Hargreaves and L. Spriet, *Exercise Metabolism* (Human Kinetics, 2006).

45 Ibid.

46 T. Bompa, *Theory and Methodology of Training* (Kendall/Hunt Publishing Company, 1994).

47 Ibid.

48 J. Blatherwick, *Over-Speed Skill Training for Hockey* (The Publishing Group, USA Hockey, 1992).

49 R. Kreider, A. Fry, and M. O'Toole, *Overtraining in Sport* (Human Kinetics, 1998).

Chapter 5

50 Hatfield, *Power: A Scientific Approach* (Contemporary Books, 1989).

51 A. V. Hill, "The Mechanics of Active Muscle." *Proceedings of the Royal Society* B141 (1953).

52 C. Dietz and B. Peterson, *Triphasic Training* (BYE Dietz Sport Enterprise, 2012).

53 I. King, *How to Write Strength-Training Programs* (King Sports Publishing, 1998/2011).

54 P. Brodal, *The Central Nervous System: Structure and Function* (Oxford University Press, 2010).

55 V. Zatsiorsky and W. Kraemer, *Science and Practice of Strength Training* (Human Kinetics, 2006).

56 D. Behm, M. Wahl, D. Button, K. Power, and K. Anderson, "Relationship between Hockey Skating Speed and Selected Performance Measures." *J Strength Cond Res* 19 no. 2 (2005): 326–331.

57 V. Zatsiorsky and W. Kraemer, *Science and Practice of Strength Training* (Human Kinetics, 2006).

58 D. Behm, M. Wahl, D. Button, K. Power, and K. Anderson, "Relationship between Hockey Skating Speed and Selected Performance Measures." *J Strength Cond Res* 19 no. 2 (2005): 326–331.

Chapter 6

59 James Smith, "Applied Sprint Training," AthleteConsulting.net, 2014.

60 Frans Bosch, *Strength Training and Coordination: An Integrative Approach* (2010 Publishers, 2015).

61 Ibid.

Chapter 7

62 I. King, *Barbells and Bullshit* (King Sport International, 2010).

63 E.L. Fox; R.W., Bowes; Foss, M.L, *The physiological basis of physical eduction and athletics* (Brown Publishers, 1989).

64 F. Dick, *Sport Training Principles* (Lepus Books, 2013).

65 T. Bompa, *Theory and Methodology of Training* (Kendall/Hunt Publishing, 1994).

66 V. Issurin, *Block Periodization 2: Fundamental Concepts and Training Design* (Ultimate Athlete Concepts, 2008).

67 M. Siff, *Facts and Fallacies of Fitness* (Denver, 2003).

68 I. King, *How to Write Strength Training Programs* (King Sports Publishing, 2011).

69 Pavel Tsatsouline, *Beyond Bodybuilding* (Dragon Door Publications, 2005).

70 A. S. Medveyev, *A System of Multi-Year Training in Weightlifting* (Livonia, MI: Sportivny Press, 1989).

71 I. King, *Legacy: Ian King's Training Innovations* (King Sports Publishing, 1980–2013).

72 Ibid.

73 T. Kurz, *Science of Sports Training* (Stadion Publishing Company, 2001).

74 Ibid.

75 T. Noakes, *The Lore of Running* (Human Kinetics, 2001).

76 R. Kreider, A. Fry, and M. O'Toole, *Overtraining in Sport* (Human Kinetics, 1998).

77 Hooper et al. 1995.

78 R. Kreider, A. Fry, and M. O'Toole, *Overtraining in Sport* (Human Kinetics, 1998).

79 D. Joyce and D. Lewindon, *High Performance Training for Sport* (Human Kinetics, 2014).

80 J. Jamieson, "Advanced Recovery and Regeneration Strategies," Midwest Performance Seminar, 2014.

Chapter 9

81 F. Batmanghelidj, *Your Body's Many Cries for Water* (Global Health Solutions, 1997).

82 D. Joyce and D. Lewindon, *High Performance Training for Sport* (Human Kinetics, 2014).

83 National Sleep Foundation, www.sleepfoundation.org.

84 SP, Sayers, DV, Harackiewicz, EA, Harman, PN, Frykman, MT, Rosenstein, "Cross-Validation of three jump power equations," *Med Sci Sports Exerc*, no. 4 (1999): 572-7.

85 T. S. Wiley, *Lights Out* (Pocket Books, 2000).

86 T. S. Wiley, *Lights Out* (Pocket Books, 2000).

87 N. Teicholz, *Big Fat Surprise* (Simon and Schuster, 2014).

88 R. Brunner, *Explosive Ergogenics for Athletes* (Ultimate Athlete Concepts, 2013).

89 R. Williams, *Biochemical Individuality* (Keats Publishing, 1998).

90 Precision Nutrition, www.precisionnutrition.com.

91 Ibid.

92 Ibid.

93 MJ, Arnaud, Metabolism of caffeine and other components of coffee (Raven Press, 1993)

94 J. Wilson, *Adrenal Fatigue* (Smart Publications, 2012).

Bonus Content

95 "Long-Term Athletic Development," Canadian Sport for Life (Canadian Sport Centres. 2010).

96 J. Joyce and D. Lewindon, *High Performance Training for Sports* (Human Kinetics, 2014).

97 www.posturalrestoration.com.

98 T. Bompa, *Theory and Methodology of Training* (Kendall/Hunt Publishing, 1994).

99 T. Bompa and D. Chambers, *Total Hockey Conditioning* (Firefly Books, 2003).

100 F. Dick, *Sport Training Principles* (Lepus Books, 2013).

Printed in the United States
By Bookmasters